T0074077

Zero-trust – An Introduction

Published 2024 by River Publishers

River Publishers

Alsbjergvej 10, 9260 Gistrup, Denmark

www.riverpublishers.com

Distributed exclusively by Routledge

605 Third Avenue, New York, NY 10017, USA

4 Park Square, Milton Park, Abingdon, Oxon OX14 4RN

Zero-trust – An Introduction / by Tom Madsen.

Routledge is an imprint of the Taylor & Francis Group, an informa business

ISBN 978-87-7022-853-4 (paperback)

ISBN 978-10-4000-705-1 (online)

ISBN 978-1-003-46458-7 (ebook master)

A Publication in the River Publishers series
RAPIDS SERIES IN DIGITAL SECURITY AND FORENSICS

Zero-trust – An Introduction

Tom Madsen

Security Architect KMD

NEW YORK AND LONDON

Contents

About the Author

Tom Madsen has 20+ years of experience in cybersecurity behind him, across many different industry segments, like finance, medical, and systems development in a secure manner. He is the author of many articles for a local Danish online magazine and is a regular writer for www.cybersecuritry-magazine.com. He has authored two other books: "The Art of War Fort Cyber Security", published by Springer, and "Security Architecture – How and Why", published by River Publishers.

Introduction

The aim of this book is to provide you with an introduction to the Zero Trust concept and provide you with information that you can use in your cybersecurity work, daily. Zero Trust as a concept in the cybersecurity industry is a new thing and it is poorly defined currently.

In this book, I will not try to nail down and define a firm definition of Zero Trust, as the concept is so new that there are as many opinions on Zero Trust, as there are people with an opinion on Zero Trust. One thing I am going to define though, is that Zerto Trust is not a product!!

Contrary to what many cybersecurity vendors are saying, buying a product does not implement Zero Trust in your infrastructure! A product can, and does help, implementing Zero Trust in your infrastructure. As I see it and remember my comment about the number of opinions on Zero Trust from earlier, Zero Trust is a way of thinking about security architecture. Using Zero Trust in designing an infrastructure, or a software application, contributes greatly to overall security of the application and infrastructure, but more on that during this book.

Below is a list of chapters and short descriptions of the content of the chapters:

- Chapter 1 – What is Zero Trust
    - In this chapter I will elaborate on some of the benefits that using zero trust can bring to your company/organization
- Chapter 2 – How to Zero Trust
    - This chapter will give you some tools and concepts to use in your zero-trust journey and cybersecurity career
- Chapter 3 – Zero Trust in the Network
    - How to design a networking infrastructure to support zero trust and some advice on tooling to help maintain and develop the zero trust in networking.

- Chapter 4 – Zero Trust identity
  - Identity management and validation is at the core of any zero-trust project. How do we use the various identities we all have in an infrastructure to zero-trust benefit?
- Chapter 5 – Cloud and Zero-trust
  - Cloud computing can be a valuable tool for implementing a zero-trust network architecture, providing flexibility, scalability, and robust security features.
- Chapter 6 – Zero Trust in OT/ICS Environments
  - OT environments are increasing their integration with IT environments, creating an ever increasing risk for compromise of the production systems in an organization. In this chapter I will extend the zero-trust concept into the OT/ICS environment and how that can benefit the security of the production systems.
- Chapter 6 – Zero-trust in 5G
  - Private 5G is being implemented in many organizations, making the security of this implementation of the utmost importance. In this chapter I will outline a zero-trust strategy for private 5G deployments.
- Chapter 8 – Zero-trust Governance
  - Without continued monitoring and maintenance, any zero-trust implementation will surely degrade over time. IN this chapter I will outline some of the monitoring that is needed to keep a zero-trust environment healthy and functioning as intended.
- Chapter 9 – Zero Trust, the next steps
  - Zero Trust is still a concept in flux. In this chapter I will try to give some advice on how-to maintain and develop an infrastructure with a zero-trust mindset.

1

Why Zero-trust

Until a few years ago, fencing systems with adequate firewalls and user ID and passwords was considered enough. But those systems were still being misused and hacked by cybercriminals using stolen credentials like user IDs and passwords to act on behalf of the exposed user. This enabled the bad actors to steal or manipulate information or even encrypt whole systems to obtain a ransom to release the encryption keys used.

Working from home, working from own devices and increased use of cloud services has added to the fact that the corporate network can no longer be regarded as the primary security perimeter. The identities that use the corporate systems are the primary perimeter, which must be secured and protected.

The answer to these developments has been to introduce *zero trust* (ZT) to the security architectures. ZT does not mean that nobody gets access; that would be harmful to any business. But access must be given after thorough verification and all communication must be encrypted. In essence, you must approach security according to the saying "Trust is fine, but control is better".

1.1 What is Zero Trust

Zero trust is difficult to pin down as a specific concept. There are as many opinions on what zero trust is as there are people with an opinion on zero trust, hence this book, which to try and build a collective understanding of zero trust.

Zero trust architecture is not an off-the-shelf product. Instead, it is a selection of tools and systems designed to enable cybersecurity paradigms that move defenses from static, network-based perimeters to focus on users, assets, and resources. The purpose of zero trust architecture is to provide authentication and authorization for a company's internal systems based on users and what devices are used.

One benefit is that this enables every employee to work from untrusted networks without the use of a VPN.

Zero trust has become the new black in the cybersecurity industry and rightly so, since zero trust, if used correctly, can bring significant security benefits to any infrastructure, weather it is an IT or an OT infrastructure. That zero trust is defined differently by different people can be seen from the definitions below. The first one is from NIST 800-207:

"Zero trust (ZT) is the term for an evolving set of cybersecurity paradigms that move defences from static, network-based perimeters to focus on users, assets, and resources"

The next one is taken from Wikipedia:

"The zero-trust security model (also, zero trust architecture, zero trust network architecture, ZTA, ZTNA), sometimes known as perimeter less security, describes an approach to the design and implementation of IT systems"

Two separate ways of defining zero trust that are, although overlapping in some ways, still approaching the world of zero trust in diverse ways. No wonder there are many opinions and definitions of zero trust.

1.2 The History of Zero Trust

Zero trust was coined as a term back in 1994 in a Ph.D. dissertation by Stephen Marsh, on an idea that "trust" can be defined mathematically. In 2003 an international group called the Jericho Forum began to study the problem, and they defined it as "de-perimiterisation" and began eliminating the idea that the internal network was a safe and protected place. Something that should have happened when the first VPN connections from outside of the network were implemented.

It took some time for the real world to catch up with the theory, but in 2009 Google created the BeyondCorp security model, which is now considered an early approach to zero trust. NIST was the first of the governmental organizations that created standards around the concept of zero trust. In 2018 they created SP 800-207 Zero Trust Architecture, updated in 2020.

NIST has decided to use zero trust as a way of looking at security architecture, something we are in full in agreement with. Zero trust should be seen as the overarching concept covering all the individual areas in an architecture, as in Figure 1.1.

Figure 1.1: Zero-trust should be seen as a full stack architecture framework covering the full spectrum of IT and applications.

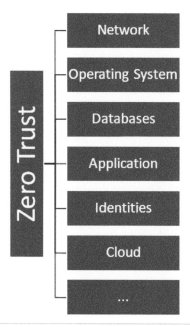

When we see zero trust as a way of designing/architecting our IT systems, zero trust becomes a concept that requires a quite broad set of skills to implement and maintain. Look at Figure 1.1 to see just a subset of the technologies we can apply zero trust to.

1.3 Why Zero Trust

With the number of breaches and the significant threat of malicious attacks on our systems, we need to approach our security measures in a way that can protect our organizations, and zero trust as a way of thinking while designing and implementing these measures will bring significant benefits to this effort.

Why has zero trust become the new black now, if the concept was coined back in 1994? Part of that answer is undoubtedly the recent pandemic we all suffered through, which disrupted the entire cybersecurity landscape. Many people were sent home to work, exacerbating the already increased use of devices and networks outside of the control systems of the enterprises. The enterprises could no longer verify that the device in use was fully updated and that the best practices defined by the organization were being followed.

The increased risks to the enterprises this brought forward, along with the needs of the end users to access everything from everywhere in the cloud and on-premises, quickly showed zero trust as a way of mitigating the risks of using unknown devices to access everything from everywhere.

So, the pandemic contributed to the sudden success of zero trust, but it is not the only factor. The massive increase in cyber-attacks has also increased the political focus on the consequences to civilian life, especially the privacy of citizens. This has meant a massive increase in the amount of regulation that organizations must show compliance with. In the EU we have the GDPR, which touches on any organization that does business within the EU. Similar legislation is being created, or has already been created, in other parts of the world. Organizations in medical or life sciences areas have the US HIPAA legislation to comply with. Organizations dealing with credit card data must comply with PCIDSS.

When we add all these together, we end up with a complex set of threats and risks that an organization must consider when managing their IT infrastructure. This makes zero trust a way of increasing the overall security of these systems; this is what has brought zero trust forward as the new black.

1.4 Operational Technology

Operational technology, or OT, is a new challenge that cybersecurity professionals must consider as part of their responsibilities. OT is the technology that runs in powerplants, controls train signals, production systems at manufacturing plants, water, electricity and many more systems. More systems than we are aware of are depending on OT technologies.

In recent years these OT systems have become integrated with the IT systems we are all familiar with. This integration means that the OT systems are now accessible from outside of the organization running the OT infrastructure, creating a risk to the OT infrastructure from hackers, and, make no mistake here, OT systems are juicy targets for hackers, especially those working for nation states. Ukraine has been suffering attacks against their OT infrastructure from Russia repeatedly over the past 5 years, to a degree where they lost access to power for several hundred thousand people for 12 hours during winter.

OT systems are not just a target for nation states. The Colonial Oil Pipeline was attacked by ransomware in May 2021, shutting down the transportation of oil from the Gulf of Mexico to the eastern states of USA. This resulted in a fuel shortage for the airlines for instance, as well as panic buying by citizens in several states from fear of running out. This just shows that attacks against OT infrastructures can have an immediate impact on society, depending on the criticality of the OT infrastructure.

I have an entire chapter on zero-trust for OT technologies and infrastructure later in the book, where I will give you an introduction to OT terminology before going into zero-trust benefits and steps for OT technology and infrastructure.

1.5 The Benefits of Zero Trust

The complexities laid out above all contribute to the rapidly increasing complexity in our infrastructures. Going the zero-trust way does not invalidate all the existing security measures we have implemented in our infrastructures, but if we approach zero-trust in a well-considered way, we can utilize the existing security tooling to implement zero trust.

Some of the core benefits can be seen in Figure 1.2.

Figure 1.2: The benefits that zero-trust will bring covers many areas where cybersecurity must be seen as important.

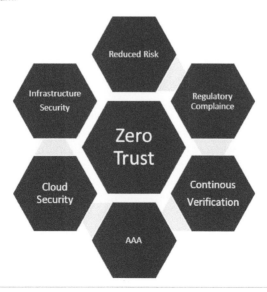

By going the zero-trust way in our infrastructure decisions, we gain all the benefits from Figure 1.2, and at the same time we will gain increased insights into our infrastructures. How? By continually verifying the accesses by our users and applications, we will also continually log these accesses and thereby gain a much deeper insight into the AAA usage in the infrastructure.

The logging and monitoring of a zero-trust architecture is of the utmost importance! If we do not continually verify that our zero-trust architecture is running as expected, we cannot be sure that we are running zero-trust as originally designed and implemented. Zero trust might seem like overkill in many situations, and the benefits difficult to identify for many organizations. This is completely understandable, since zero-trust is an all-compassing concept, touching on all areas of IT.

Advice on how to approach a zero-trust project will be detailed in the next chapter, but before we leave behind this introductory chapter, I would like to touch upon how such a project might be received by the end users. Zero trust is an aggressive way to name a project. I have a client that has run into pushbacks from the end users. Someone who has been working for an organization for years, who is suddenly seen as a zero-trust entity, will understandably ask why that is the case. I have seen zero-trust projects called maximize trust instead, but we should still expect the users to ask questions, since they will see these projects as questioning their integrity.

Getting the end users aboard zero-trust projects will require a great deal of communication to make them understand the benefits, not just for the organization, but for them as well. For instance, the possibilities for them being hacked decreases with a zero-trust architecture.

1.6 Outro

Lastly, the technologies we are using for the examples in this book are from Microsoft and Cisco. This does not constitute a recommendation, or an attempt to convey that these vendors are the only ones that do zero trust. These are the technologies that we are familiar with and are using in our daily work. If you are using networking technology from the likes of HPE, Juniper or Palo Alto Networks, the same recommendations and design advice apply to these vendors, and these vendors can deliver the same level of zero trust in their technologies as Cisco.

If your main software vendor is not Microsoft, but Oracle or SAP, your main cloud provider Oracle or Salesforce, then yes, they can deliver the same level of assurance for zero trust as Microsoft can. The steps will be different of course, but there will be no difference in the level of zero trust, if done right.

2

How to Zero Trust

In this chapter, I will give you some pointers on how to begin a zero-trust project, but first let's begin with a figure that shows the size and complexity of any zero-trust project. Look at Figure 2.1.

Figure 2.1: Zero-trust requires that the user in the upper left corner gets validated through the entire flow, before getting access to the application in the lower right.

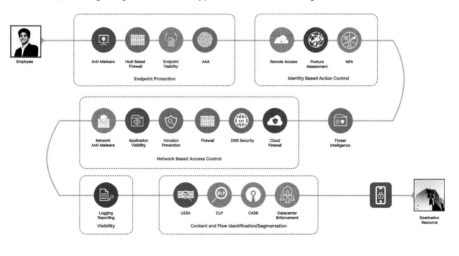

We have a user in the top left, trying to access a resource on the lower right. The flow demonstrates the possible checks a user must go through to access the resource. Fortunately, many of these checks and systems are automated in nature, with no direct effect on the user experience, but it does demonstrate the complexity of a zero-trust project.

A zero-trust project is an all or nothing effort. We cannot implement zero trust for a subset of the infrastructure or systems, making zero trust a huge, and often long term, effort in most organizations, but the overall benefits to the cybersecurity of the organization should not be underestimated when deciding on starting a zero-trust journey.

2.1 The Politics of Zero Trust

Before beginning a zero-trust project, there are some political issues to consider. For instance, when you announce a zero-trust project, there will be some users that push back against it, not necessarily because they are opposed to the effort, but because they see the project as a signal, they are untrusted. It might sound like this: I have been here for 10 years, why am I suddenly untrusted? A fair response all thing considered; I am bringing this up to make you aware that zero-trust can be seen as aggressive by the user community in an organization.

You might ask, is that really a thing, push back from the users because of the name? Yes, I have clients that have experienced this exact response! So, bringing the users on board with a zero-trust project is important from the very beginning, as well as communication that they are still trusted, even when we are implementing a zero-trust architecture in the infrastructure.

This probable push back is also a reason for anchoring the zero-trust project at the most senior level of the leadership in the organization. IT cannot implement a zero-trust project without the support of the senior leadership.

While zero trust originated in the field of cybersecurity, it has also gained attention in the realm of politics and governance, particularly in discussions surrounding national security, privacy, and data protection.

2.2 Where to Begin

Before beginning a zero-trust journey we must assess where the organization is, maturity wise, regarding the overall cybersecurity. First, let us look at the three pillars of zero-trust in Figure 2.2.

Figure 2.2: Most of the advice in this figure has been important for years, but with zero-trust it gets incorporated into a framework.

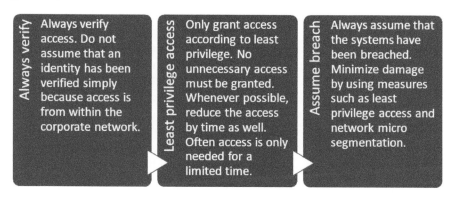

Identities are the center of the basic pillars. These are not limited to persons (employees, contractors, customers, etc.) but also technical identities like IOT devices, robots, and applications.

Basically, there are as many implementations of zero-trust architectures as there are vendors who offer solutions to implement zero trust. However, zero-trust architectures do have some common features and core components of which the most central are shown in Figure 2.3.

Figure 2.3: NIST provides good advice in their 800-207 document, the three points above are especially important to a good zero-trust implementation.

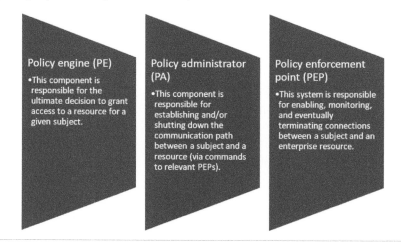

These definitions are from the NIST 800-207 standard, issued by the National Institute of Standard and Technology under the US Department of Commerce in 2020 as a reference architecture for zero-trust architectures.

There are examples of each of the above terms and technologies in the chapters on zero trust in the network and identities, as used for zero-trust purposes. In many cases companies and organizations will already have systems in place that can be used as PE, PA and PEP in a zero-trust project, making a zero-trust project a matter of allocating resources for the design and implementation of zero trust in the infrastructure and not necessarily a matter of investing in new hardware and software for the project. But make no mistake here, the cost of a zero-trust project does not come from any investments in hardware and software, it comes from the amount of time and resources needed to assess and implement zero trust in an existing infrastructure.

The focus of a zero-trust architecture is on authentication, authorization and minimizing implicit trust zones while minimizing delays caused by authentication. In the abstract model below, which is borrowed from the NIST 800-207 standard, a user needs access to an enterprise resource. Access is granted through the policy decision point (PDP) and the corresponding policy enforcement point (PEP). The PDP must ensure that the subject is authentic and is authorized to carry out the request. The implicit trust zone represents an area where all the entities are trusted at least to the level of the last PDP/PEP gateway.

The NIST 800-207 standard describes three variations in how zero trust can be implemented. The variations, which supplement one another, are zero-trust architecture using:

- Enhanced identity governance
- Micro-segmentation
- Network infrastructure and software defined perimeters.

Beginning a zero-trust project can seem overwhelming, but it is important to start with a clear plan and a well-defined scope. Here are some steps to consider when beginning a zero-trust project:

1. Define your project scope: Clearly define the scope of your project, including what resources and services will be included and what level of security you are aiming for.
2. Identify critical assets: Identify the most critical assets that need to be protected, such as sensitive data or key infrastructure components. This will help you prioritize your security efforts and allocate resources effectively.
3. Assess your current security posture: Conduct a thorough assessment of your current security posture to identify potential vulnerabilities and areas for improvement.

4. Develop a zero-trust architecture: Develop a zero-trust architecture that is tailored to your specific needs and aligns with your project scope. This should include a detailed plan for access control, network segmentation, and data protection.
5. Implement security controls: Implement the necessary security controls to support your zero-trust architecture. This may include multi-factor authentication, encryption, and access controls.
6. Monitor and adjust: Continuously monitor and adjust your security controls as needed to ensure that they are effective and that your zero-trust architecture remains up to date.
7. Train your staff: Train your staff on the principles of zero-trust security and how to implement best practices to maintain a secure environment.

Remember that zero-trust security is an ongoing process, not a one-time project. It requires constant monitoring, adjustment, and refinement to ensure that your organization is protected against emerging threats.

2.2.1 Assessment

Before beginning a zero-trust project, you should perform an inventory and risk assessment. The assessment is independent of what tool is used and must always be carried out as part of a successful IAM implementation.

All identities must be assessed. Employees are obvious, but how about contractors, robots, and technical accounts? How do you register employees and contractors? In many cases this data is derived from the HR system, but the data quality needs to be assessed. There are examples of IAM projects that have exceeded the expected timeframe by 50% due to bad data quality from the HR system and as such an IAM/IGA program may in some cases require an HR cleanup.

For each application in use in your organization it is important to assess the data shown in Figure 2.4.

Surprises frequently surface during the assessment of applications. With easily accessible software- as-a-service (SaaS) solutions, business units often run part of the business in an autonomous manner, without official knowledge or approval from IT. Known as "shadow IT", these applications often contain critical company data, and the access to these or the business data within is seldomly managed according to the organization's standards.

Make no mistake here, doing a full assessment of the IT infrastructure is by no means an easy job. It requires good documentation, a rare occurrence, and an open dialogue with the various business departments to identify all SaaS solutions they might have procured outside of the knowledge of IT.

Figure 2.4: Assessing the data used and created in an organization is critical to a successful implementation of zero-trust.

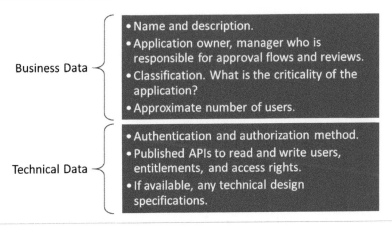

Business Data
- Name and description.
- Application owner, manager who is responsible for approval flows and reviews.
- Classification. What is the criticality of the application?
- Approximate number of users.

Technical Data
- Authentication and authorization method.
- Published APIs to read and write users, entitlements, and access rights.
- If available, any technical design specifications.

Where do we start such an assessment? Fortunately, there are many frameworks that can be used as a basis for an assessment. Some of them are:

- CIS 18
- ISO 2700x
- COBIT
- NIST.

All of them list controls that can be used as the basis for a questionnaire for an overall IT infrastructure assessment. In the case of CIS 18, you can even download an Excel sheet with the individual controls and a list of sub-areas of the main 18 control areas for free. ISO 2700x and COBIT will cost you some money, but they are both well worth the cost, not just for a zero-trust project.

2.2.2 Classify

Classifying what you have is important, both systems and data. This way, you will know where to focus and what to protect the most. There are usually standard sets of classification parameters that can be used, but your organization may also choose its own set of classifications. Every classification must have a risk weight assigned to it. When applications and access rights have been classified with risk weights, you are able to conduct risk-based reviews on identities, systems and applications with high-risk profiles because they have access to high-risk systems. There are some crucial questions that should be answered for the application and access rights. These are given in Figure 2.5.

Figure 2.5: Like assessing the data from earlier in the chapter, assessing the access rights of the users and the level of their rights is critical to zero-trust.

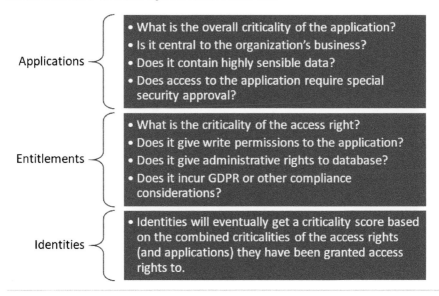

2.2.3 Access rights

A frequent problem is that users have too many access rights, which leads to the risk that a compromised user will allow for an intruder to gain access to major parts of the organization's data and applications.

Zero trust access rights refer to the principle of granting access privileges based on the specific needs and context of individual users, devices and applications, rather than relying on broad trust assumptions. In a zero-trust model, access rights are carefully managed and continuously evaluated, regardless of whether the user is inside or outside the network perimeter.

Here are some key aspects of zero-trust access rights:

- Least privilege: Users and entities are granted the minimum level of access necessary to perform their intended tasks. This principle ensures that each user only has access to the resources and data required for their specific role, minimizing the potential impact of a compromised account.
- Continuous authentication: Instead of relying solely on a one-time authentication event, zero trust emphasizes continuous authentication and authorization. This means that users' identities and access rights are re-evaluated and verified at each access attempt, considering factors such as user behavior, device health, and network conditions.

- Granular access controls: Zero trust promotes fine-grained access controls, enabling organizations to define specific permissions and restrictions for different resources, applications, and data. Access can be based on factors such as user roles, location, time of access, device type, and security posture.
- Multi-factor authentication (MFA): Implementing MFA is a critical component of zero-trust access. By requiring users to provide multiple forms of authentication (such as passwords, biometrics, or tokens), the risk of unauthorized access through stolen or compromised credentials is reduced.

In a zero-trust architecture, dynamic access controls are invoked on the fly based on criteria, which are current at the time of authentication:

Rule-based access control. The various vendors have different implementations of the policy engine, which enforces rule-based access control, and may even be carried out by the application itself. As an example of the latter, Salesforce enables users logging on to Salesforce.com to restrict their access to certain IP-addresses or during specified hours during the day.

Attribute-based access control. Attribute-based access control is dynamically adapting the access based on certain attributes associated with the identity. The attributes can be of any type, such as location, time, activity and user credentials. An example could be that a manager is allowed to approve expenses, just not their own. An attribute-based access control can also be that you cannot access the application from outside the office location unless you use a company PC or, every 30 days, you must use a two-factor login method to get access to the application. Static access is defined as the accesses that are given due to your job role. Often different access rights are combined according to specific job roles, i.e., "I work in the sales department and thus have access to the CRM application".

Role-based access control. Role-based access control (RBAC) describes the various job roles that require access to information systems and describe the accesses rights that are necessary to perform these job roles. Then finally, grant access based on job roles instead of individual access rights in various applications. The composition of roles should be verified periodically. In all organizations the application landscape is usually under development and changes should be reflected in the roles. You may also be asked to document the composition of job roles during internal or external audits. Any professional IAM tool in the market will include functionality to define rules for separation of duties (SoD).

Separation of duties. In SoD you define so-called "toxic combinations" of access rights. A toxic combination of access rights could be "approving timecards" and "having custody of pay checks". In essence, the concept behind SoD is to have more than one person required to complete certain critical tasks. It is an administrative control used by organizations to prevent fraud, sabotage, theft, misuse of information, and other security compromises.

2.2.4 Challenges

At the beginning of this chapter, I said that a zero-trust project was an all or nothing project., That is still the case but there are challenges, especially in large organizations with large and often legacy infrastructures.

- Legacy infrastructure: Many organizations have existing network architectures and legacy systems that may not easily align with the principles of zero trust. Retrofitting these systems or transitioning to new infrastructure can be complex and require careful planning.
- Complexity and scalability: Zero-trust implementations can be complex due to the need for granular access controls, continuous authentication, and network segmentation. Managing and scaling these systems across a large organization can be challenging and require significant effort and resources.
- User experience: Introducing strict authentication and authorization processes can potentially impact the user experience. Balancing security with convenience is crucial to ensure that employees and users do not face excessive friction when accessing resources.
- Visibility and monitoring: Zero-trust architectures require robust monitoring and visibility tools to track user activity, identify potential threats, and respond to incidents effectively. Organizations need to invest in appropriate monitoring solutions and processes to gain real-time insights into network traffic and access patterns.
- Change management: Implementing zero trust often involves a significant shift in mindset and cultural change within an organization. Users, administrators, and stakeholders need to understand the new security paradigm and the reasons behind it. Adequate training and change management efforts are essential to foster acceptance and cooperation.
- Third-Party Integration: Organizations often rely on external vendors, partners, and cloud service providers. Integrating these entities into a zero-trust framework can be challenging, as their security practices and capabilities may vary. Ensuring consistent security standards and collaboration with third parties is crucial.
- Cost: Implementing a zero-trust architecture may require investments in new technologies, infrastructure upgrades, and security solutions. Organizations must carefully assess the costs involved and balance them against the potential benefits and risks.

We all know that we should keep our software and hardware up to date with patches and hardware platforms, but the reality is that this is often not possible in complex infrastructures, where legacy hardware is incapable of strong encryption for instance. This is the unfortunate reality in many organizations, both because of compliance issues, like in the life science sector, or public transport sectors.

For public transport using trains, in Denmark at least, there are laws governing the installation and use of new hardware in the trains. Because trains are used for decades, this means that some of the trains in Denmark are still using WEP for the wireless security, something we left behind as insecure in the late 1990s.

Banks still have legacy code running on mainframes developed in COBOL or PL/1 that cannot be easily updated, since COBOL and PL/1 programmers are largely retired by now. Some organizations still have business critical applications running developed in Visual Basic 5/6 in some cases. How ever much we would like this reality to be different, we must take it into account in a zero-trust project. We might not be able to spread zero-trust into legacy systems, but we can, as part of the process, mitigate the risks presented by legacy hardware and software.

2.3 The Benefits

Having the infrastructure hardened and designed as a foundation for a zero-trust journey, will serve as a source of the overall security of the organization, not just the zero-trust projects. If you have reasonably new hardware/software in your infrastructure, you can use the existing functionality in the infrastructure to build the foundation for zero-trust. A zero-trust project does not necessarily mean a big investment in new hardware and software.

Doing an assessment on the existing infrastructure before investing in new HW/SW for a zero-trust project will undoubtedly result in better utilization of the existing HW/SW and money being saved. The traditional steps for securing the network, segmentation, and authentication are still applicable in a zero-trust networking architecture.

What I am trying to convey here is that a zero-trust project does not mean a big capital investment from the get-go! Any reasonably up to date infrastructure can be used as a basis for a zero-trust implementation. Some of the core benefits of a zero-trust project at the networking infrastructure level are:

1. Improved security: A zero-trust hardened infrastructure provides a more robust and secure environment by reducing the attack surface and implementing strong access controls and authentication protocols.
2. Protection against advanced threats: By assuming that all traffic is potentially malicious, a zero-trust infrastructure can protect against advanced threats such as malware, ransomware, and zero-day attacks.

3. Greater visibility: A zero-trust infrastructure provides greater visibility into network activity, enabling administrators to quickly identify and respond to security incidents.

4. Better compliance: A zero-trust infrastructure can help organizations meet regulatory compliance requirements by implementing strong access controls and data protection measures.

5. Simplified management: A zero-trust infrastructure can simplify network management by implementing a unified policy across all resources and services, reducing the complexity of security management.

6. Reduced risk of insider threats: Zero-trust security reduces the risk of insider threats by limiting access to sensitive resources and requiring additional verification for privileged users.

7. Improved user experience: By implementing strong authentication and access controls, a zero-trust infrastructure can improve the user experience by reducing the risk of unauthorized access and data breaches.

What we are trying to achieve is the upper right corner of Figure 2.6, no easy task but well worth the effort!

Figure 2.6: The sweet spot for any security implementation is in the upper right corner, just keep in mind that data and applications can be critical enough that we might have to limit usability!

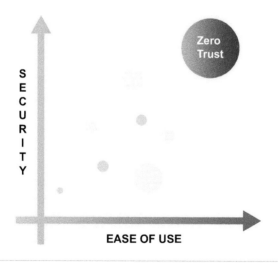

2.4 A summary

A quick summary of the steps involved in implementing zero trust is:

1. Identify and categorize assets: Identify the critical assets, resources, and data that need protection. Categorize them based on their sensitivity and importance.

2. Define access policies: Determine access policies based on the principle of least privilege. Define who should have access to specific resources, applications, and data, and under what conditions.

3. Implement strong authentication: Deploy multi-factor authentication (MFA) mechanisms to strengthen user authentication. Require users to provide multiple forms of verification, such as passwords, biometrics, or tokens.

4. Enable continuous monitoring: Implement real-time monitoring and logging to track user activity, network traffic, and access attempts. Use this data to detect anomalies, identify potential threats, and respond promptly.

5. Segment the network: Implement network segmentation to create isolated zones or compartments. Separate critical assets, applications, and data into different segments to restrict lateral movement and limit the potential impact of a breach.

1. Embrace micro-segmentation: Apply micro-segmentation techniques to further segment the network into smaller, granular segments. This allows for even more precise access controls and containment of potential threats.

2. Adopt a zero-trust architecture: Transition from a perimeter-based security model to a zero-trust architecture. This involves removing the implicit trust assumptions and implementing continuous authentication and authorization mechanisms for every access request, both within and outside the network perimeter.

3. Implement least privilege access: Grant access rights based on the principle of least privilege. Users should only have access to the resources they need to perform their specific roles and tasks.

4. Monitor and analyze behavior: Utilize behavior analytics and anomaly detection to identify unusual user behavior or suspicious activities. Continuously monitor and analyze user behavior to detect potential insider threats or compromised accounts.

5. Educate and train employees: Provide comprehensive training and awareness programs to educate employees about the zero-trust model, the importance of security, and their roles and responsibilities in maintaining a secure environment.

6. Regularly assess and update security controls: Continuously evaluate and update security controls, access policies, and technologies to adapt to evolving threats and vulnerabilities.

Remember that implementing zero trust is a journey rather than a one-time task. It requires ongoing commitment, collaboration, and adaptation to ensure the security of your organization's assets and data.

Lastly, none of the above steps can stand alone in a zero-trust project, but they are all integral to the success of the overall implementation and maintenance of a zero-trust project!

3

Zero Trust – The Networking Level

This chapter we will focus strictly on the networking level. By that I mean subjects like networking design, network access, micro segmentation, MFA and more. The network is a vital component in any IT infrastructure. Even if your company is in the cloud, the network is the component that makes it possible for you to use the cloud. Unfortunately, many organizations are not using the security options present in a well-maintained network.

In this chapter we will, again, use the figure from the beginning of Chapter 2 (Figure 3.1):

Figure 3.1: This figure is just as relevant for zero-trust at the networking level as it is for the other layers in a zero-trust implementation.

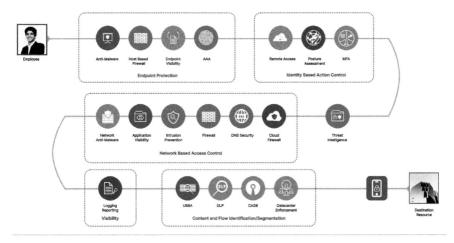

You might think that the figure might suit a more overall approach to zero-trust, and not a networking focused one, but you would be wrong. Remember, the network is the foundation of all of the zero-trust architecture that is needed for a zero-trust implementation. Remember, the user in the upper left corner needs to use the network to access the application in the lower right.

The traditional approach to security was based on the concept of "trust but verify." The weakness of this approach is that once someone was authenticated, they were considered trusted and could move laterally to access sensitive data and systems that should have been off-limits.

Zero trust principles change this to "never trust, always verify." A zero-trust architecture doesn't aim to make a system trusted or secure, but rather to eliminate the concept of trust altogether. Zero trust security models assume that an attacker is always present in the environment. Trust is never granted unconditionally or permanently but must be continually evaluated.

The development of the zero trust approach is in response to the traditional methods of how enterprise assets, resources and data were accessed over the years. In the early days of computing, companies were able to protect their data by using firewalls and other security technologies that set up a "secure perimeter" around the data. Much like a castle wall in medieval times, these technologies helped protect what was inside, mostly.

But the perimeter changed, rapidly with the onset of Covid 19, as employees, contractors, and business partners began working remotely – accessing resources via cloud-based networks or with personally owned devices that couldn't always be verified as completely secured. In addition, the deployment of Internet of Things (IoT) devices (to be touched upon more deeply in Chapter 5), which often had automatic access to network resources, increased.

To allow employees, partners and contractors access to network resources, a zero-trust architecture requires a combination of technologies, including identity management, asset management, application authentication, access control, network segmentation, and threat intelligence.

The balancing act of zero trust is to enhance security without sacrificing the user experience, that magical upper right quadrant from Figure 2.6. Once authenticated and authorized, a user is given access, but only to the resources they need in order to perform their job. If a device or resource is compromised, zero trust ensures that the damage can be contained.

The good news for many companies is that they likely already possess most of the zero-trust enabling technologies. In adopting a zero-trust approach, companies will more likely need to adopt and enforce new policies, rather than install new hardware.

As mentioned, the network is the foundation for all the infrastructure a modern business needs in its operation (Figure 3.2). This makes the network a vital component in a zero-trust journey since the rest of the infrastructure rests on the security the network provides.

Figure 3.2: The network is the foundation for implementing zero-trust up through the stack.

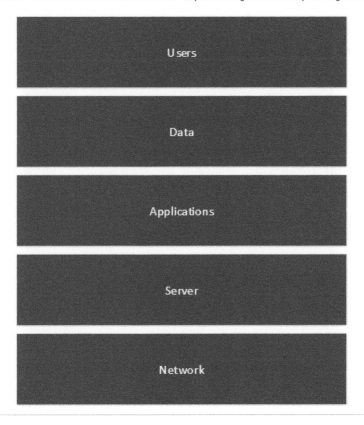

Zero trust is a strategic approach to security that centres on the concept of eliminating trust from an organization's network architecture. Trust is neither binary nor permanent. It can no longer be assumed that internal entities are trustworthy, that they can be directly managed to reduce security risks, or that checking them once is enough. The zero-trust model of security prompts you to question your assumptions of trust at every access attempt.

3.1 Zero-trust Security Frameworks

Figure 3.3: There are various ways of looking at zero-trust. This figure is relating Cisco, CISA and NIST. One is not better than the other, use the one that first your needs!

Cisco	NIST	CISA – Cybersecurity and Infrastructure Security Agency	Common
User & Device Security	Users	Identity	Visibility & Analytics
	Devices	Device	Automation &
Network & Cloud Security	Networks/Hybrid	Network/	Orchestration
	Multi-Cloud	Environment	Governance
Application and Data Security	Applications	Application Workload	
	Data	Data	

This chapter is partly focused on the Cisco Zero Trust Framework with the User and Device Security, Application and Data Security, and Network and Cloud Security pillars (Figure 3.3).

3.2 Approach

Before you start deploying a zero-trust architecture, there are several basic rules that must be followed across the company for the system to work.

- All data sources, computing services, and devices are considered resources. Even employee-owned devices must be considered a resource if they can access enterprise-owned resources.
- All communication should be secured, regardless of the network location.
- Access to resources is granted on a per-session basis, and with the least privileges needed to complete a task.
- Access to resources is determined through a dynamic policy that includes the state of a client's identity and application.
- An enterprise must monitor and measure the integrity and security posture of all owned and associated assets.
- Authentication and authorization are strictly enforced before access is allowed and can be subject to change.
- An organization needs to collect as much information as possible about the current state of their assets, network infrastructure, communications, end users and devices in order to improve their security posture.

Once a resource has been identified as protected, a company needs to set up "checkpoints" that are responsible for the decision to allow or deny access. There are three main components, based on terms coined by NIST in its Zero Trust Architecture document, 800-207 from August 2020.

- **Policy engine (PE):** A policy engine (PE) is responsible for making the decision to grant or deny access to a resource (see Section 3.4.3.1).
- **Policy administrator (PA):** The PA is responsible for establishing or shutting down the communication path between a requestor (either a person or machine) and the resource (data, service, application).
- **Policy enforcement point (PEP):** The PEP enables, monitors, and eventually terminates connections between a requestor and the resource.

Additional systems can contribute input and/or policy rules, including CDM systems, or the Cisco DNA Center mentioned in Section 3.4.3.2, industry compliance systems (making sure that these systems remain compliant with regulatory agencies), threat intelligence services (giving information about newly identified malware, software flaws, or other reported attacks), network and system activity logs, and identity management systems.

Many of these systems feed data into a trust algorithm that helps make the ultimate decision for the request to access network resources. The trust algorithm considers data from the requestor as well as several other metrics as part of its decision. Examples of questions include, but are not limited to:

- Who is this person? Is it a real person, a service account or a machine?
- Have they requested this before?
- What device are they using?
- Is the OS version updated and patched?

In Figure 3.4 I have designed a common situation for many companies, especially those of an international nature. There is headquarters, possibly more than one, with many sub-offices scattered around the country or world. In cases where the company has been buying other companies, the infrastructure will be a complex set of infrastructures from different vendors and different design philosophies, making the overall infrastructure situation complex and difficult to manage.

The situation described above might seem like an unreasonable situation, but it is the reality for many companies around the world. Of course, there are situations where a zero-trust project will have an easier go at it, but you should expect those to be few and far between. So, how do we begin a zero-trust project in such a situation?

Every company is different, so the way they approach zero trust will vary. Here are a few common scenarios:

Figure 3.4: Keep in mind that many organizations are distributed across a country and even the world. Zero-trust in such a situation is a major effort.

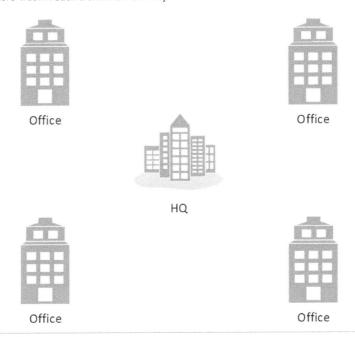

- **An enterprise with satellite offices** (like above): Companies that have employees working at remote locations, or remote workers, would likely need to have a PE/PA hosted as a cloud service.
- **Multi cloud, or cloud 2 cloud enterprises:** Companies that use multiple cloud providers (an ever-increasing number of enterprises!) might see a situation where an application is hosted on a cloud service that is separate from the data source.
- **Enterprises with non-employee or contractor access:** For on-site visitors or contracted service providers that need limited access, a zero-trust architecture would also likely deploy the PE and PA as a hosted cloud service, or on the LAN, in non-cloud cases.

3.3 Segmentation/Micro Segmentation

Segmentation has been a mantra for security at the networking level for many years now and the importance of segmentation has only increased with criticality of IT to the businesses and organizations. The original goal of segmentation was to limit the occurrences of broadcast storms, but it has migrated away from the core purpose to be aimed at controlling the kinds of traffic allowed between departments. Does HR need to access finance resources, for instance, or does the receptionist need access to RnD resources? Those are the kinds of use cases I see among my clients on a nearly daily basis.

The next use case for segmentation is controlling the kinds of traffic allowed on each of the network segments. See Figure 3.5.

Figure 3.5: Segmentation is a core part of zero-trust at the networking level of an infrastructure.

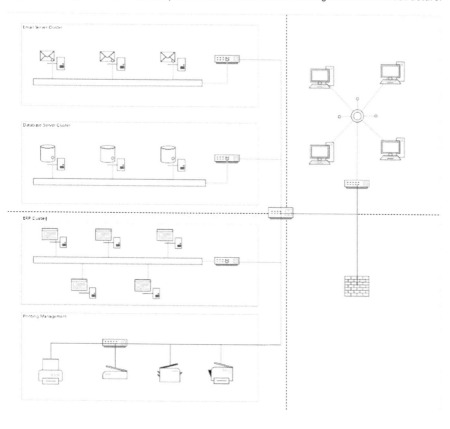

In this figure the various workloads are divided into clusters, in a real organization, there will be many more clusters than you see here, this is just to provide a foundation. By creating the VLAN segmentation like in Figure 3.5, we can control traffic between the clusters, and control what kind of traffic is allowed on the VLAN's in each cluster.

The ERP cluster will undoubtedly need to communicate with the database cluster, but should the traffic coming from the ERP cluster be allowed non database traffic? Maybe, but by segmenting the server workloads into discrete clusters, we can control, and monitor, the traffic, and protocols that we allow between the clusters. This provides us with an enormous amount of insight into our traffic patterns, while at the same time we are limiting the attack surface that a malicious attacker can utilize to compromise the business or organization.

3.4 Software Defined Networking/Software Defined Access

Software defined networking and software defined access are concepts that are still new to networking technologies and infrastructures, so let's begin this section by defining SDN and SDA, and their relations to zero-trust, before moving on.

3.4.1 SDN

Software-defined networking (SDN) is a network architecture that separates the control plane and data plane of a network, enabling centralized management and programmability of network resources. SDN can be used to implement a zero-trust network architecture by providing greater control and visibility into network traffic and enabling more granular access controls.

One of the key benefits of SDN in the context of zero-trust networking is that it enables administrators to implement dynamic access controls that can adapt to changing threat conditions. By dynamically controlling access based on real-time network traffic analysis and user behavior, SDN can provide a more fine-grained approach to access control that is better suited to the zero-trust model.

Additional benefits are:

- Centralized control: SDN enables centralized management and control of network resources, allowing administrators to have a holistic view and make configuration changes from a centralized controller. This simplifies network management and improves efficiency.
- Agility and flexibility: SDN allows for dynamic network configuration and rapid provisioning of network services. It enables organizations to quickly adapt to changing business needs, scale their network infrastructure, and deploy new services or applications faster.
- Network automation: SDN enables network automation through programmable interfaces and APIs. This simplifies the deployment and management of network services, reduces human errors, and improves operational efficiency.

- Cost efficiency: SDN can help reduce costs by optimizing network resource utilization, enabling better traffic engineering, and supporting the use of commodity hardware. It allows organizations to leverage cost-effective solutions and avoid vendor lock-in.
- Enhanced network visibility: SDN provides granular visibility into network traffic and allows for real-time monitoring and analysis. This visibility enables better troubleshooting, performance optimization, and security threat detection.

SDN can also facilitate micro-segmentation of the network, which is a key component of zero-trust architecture. By dividing the network into smaller segments, administrators can apply more granular access controls and reduce the attack surface of the network.

Another benefit of SDN in the context of zero-trust networking is that it enables administrators to deploy security policies across the network more easily and efficiently. By centralizing network management and programmability, administrators can more easily implement security policies that apply to all network resources and services.

Overall, SDN can be a valuable tool for implementing zero-trust networking, providing greater control, visibility, and security for network resources and services. By leveraging the programmability and centralized management capabilities of SDN, administrators can more easily implement a zero-trust architecture and protect against advanced threats.

Software defined networking (SDN) and zero-trust are two separate but related concepts in the field of computer networking and security.

SDN refers to an approach to networking that separates the control plane (which determines how data packets are forwarded) from the data plane (which forwards the packets). This allows for more flexible and programmable networks, since the control plane can be managed using software-defined controllers rather than hard-coded into individual network devices.

Zero-trust, on the other hand, is a security model that assumes that all network traffic (including traffic within a private network) is potentially malicious and should be treated with suspicion. Under a zero-trust model, access to network resources is granted on a need-to-know basis and is constantly re-evaluated based on contextual factors such as user identity, device security posture, and network location.

The two concepts are related because SDN can be used to implement a zero-trust security model. By using a software-defined controller to manage access control policies, network administrators can more easily adapt to changing security requirements and ensure that only authorized users and devices are granted access to sensitive resources.

For example, an SDN-enabled network might use a centralized policy controller to dynamically assign access privileges based on contextual factors such as user identity and device security posture. If a user attempts to access a sensitive resource from an unsecured device, the policy controller could deny the request or redirect the user to a secure device or network segment. This kind of dynamic access control is difficult to implement using traditional network security methods but can be relatively straightforward using SDN.

SDN is an architecture designed to make a network more flexible and easier to manage. SDN centralizes management by abstracting the control plane from the data forwarding function in the discrete networking devices. For SDA the definition is more aligned with a zero-trust way of thinking.

3.4.2 SDA

Software-defined access (SD-Access) is a networking architecture that enables dynamic network segmentation, role-based access control, and policy automation. SD-Access is an extension of the software-defined networking (SDN) paradigm that aims to simplify and automate access control by using a centralized policy engine to enforce network policies.

Zero-trust security model and SD-Access share the same philosophy of assuming that all network traffic is potentially malicious and should not be trusted by default. Both approaches seek to minimize the attack surface of the network and provide granular access control to network resources.

By using SD-Access in conjunction with a zero-trust security model, an organization can ensure that only authorized users and devices are allowed to access sensitive resources. SD-Access can provide dynamic network segmentation, which means that network resources can be isolated into different segments based on the security requirements of the applications and data. Access to these segments can be granted on a need-to-know basis and can be constantly re-evaluated based on contextual factors such as user identity, device security posture, and network location.

In an SD-Access and zero-trust architecture, the network can automatically adjust access policies based on contextual information such as location, device type, and user identity. For example, a user attempting to access a sensitive application from an untrusted device may be denied access or required to authenticate using multi-factor authentication.

SD-Access gives network architects the tools to orchestrate key business functions like onboarding, secure segmentation, IoT integration, and guest access. SD-Access automates user and device policy for any application across the wireless and wired network via a single network fabric.

SD-Access benefits are:

- Simplified network management: SD-Access centralizes network management through policy-based automation. It enables administrators to define and enforce access policies from a central controller, simplifying network provisioning, configuration, and troubleshooting.
- Network segmentation: SD-Access allows for granular network segmentation based on user roles, device types, or other contextual factors. This segmentation enhances security by isolating different segments and controlling the flow of network traffic.
- Automated policy enforcement: SD-Access automates the enforcement of access policies, ensuring consistent application of security controls across the network. This reduces the risk of misconfiguration or human errors and improves overall security posture.
- Enhanced visibility and analytics: SD-Access provides greater visibility into network traffic, user behavior, and application performance. This visibility enables proactive monitoring, faster troubleshooting, and better insights for optimizing network performance and security.
- Scalability and flexibility: SD-Access is designed to scale and adapt to changing business needs. It supports dynamic provisioning, easy scalability, and the ability to integrate new devices and technologies seamlessly.

3.4.3 Tooling

I begin this section by defining and describing the toolset from Cisco I am using later in this chapter for the actual implementation of zero-trust in the network.

3.4.3.1 Cisco ISE (Identity Services Engine)

The Cisco Identity Services Engine (ISE) is a network access control and security policy management platform that can be used to implement a zero-trust security model.

The ISE is designed to provide visibility and control over network access by authenticating users and devices, enforcing access policies, and providing endpoint compliance checks. ISE can integrate with various other Cisco security technologies, such as Cisco Secure Firewall, to provide comprehensive network security.

In a zero-trust security model, ISE can play a critical role in ensuring that only authorized users and devices are granted access to network resources. ISE can provide policy enforcement for dynamic network segmentation, micro-segmentation, and context-based access control. This means that access to network resources can be granted based on factors such as user identity, device security posture, and network location, rather than simply allowing access based on a user's network credentials.

ISE can also provide identity and access management capabilities, such as multi-factor authentication, single sign-on (SSO), and user provisioning. These features can help to simplify access control and improve the user experience while maintaining a strong security posture.

Additionally, ISE can provide continuous monitoring and threat detection capabilities to identify anomalous behavior and potential security threats in real-time. This can help organizations to quickly respond to security incidents and mitigate potential damage.

3.4.3.2 Cisco DNA Center

The Cisco DNA Center is a software-based network management platform that can be used to implement a zero-trust security model.

With the DNA Center, administrators can define policies for network access based on a user's identity, device type, location, and other contextual factors. These policies can be enforced across the network using software-defined networking (SDN) capabilities, such as network segmentation and micro-segmentation. This approach allows administrators to create a zero-trust environment, where all traffic is treated as potentially malicious and access to network resources is granted on a need-to-know basis.

Some of the key capabilities of the DNA Center that enable a zero-trust security model include:

- Software-defined access (SD-Access): This is an automated network segmentation technology that allows administrators to define and enforce policies for user and device access. By using SD-Access, administrators can segment the network based on user groups, device types, and other contextual factors, and apply different policies to each segment.
- Identity services engine (ISE) integration: The DNA Center can be integrated with Cisco ISE to provide network access control (NAC) and identity and access management (IAM) capabilities. ISE can authenticate users and devices, enforce access policies, and provide endpoint compliance checks.
- Analytics and assurance: The DNA Center provides real-time visibility into network traffic, allowing administrators to detect anomalies and potential security threats. This feature can help organizations quickly respond to security incidents and mitigate potential damage.

In summary, the Cisco DNA Center provides a comprehensive set of capabilities that can be used to implement a zero-trust security model. By using software-defined networking and integration with Cisco ISE, organizations can create a dynamic, policy-driven environment where access to network resources is granted on a need-to-know basis. Additionally, the analytics and assurance capabilities of the DNA Center can help to detect and mitigate potential security threats in real-time.

Using the software defined approach outlined above, we can create policies at the networking level, controlling and managing the accesses that the users are given on the network. From Cisco two tools are used for this:

- Cisco ISE

    o   Access control to both the network and the networking infrastructure
    o   BYOD
    o   Guest Access.

- Cisco DNA Center

    o   Automation
    o   Analytics
    o   Virtualization.

Using these two solutions, we can control who has access and what kinds of access they are given on the network. Cisco ISE will be mentioned in the next section as well, on multi-factor authentication.

Using the Cisco ISE and DNA Center, we can create the policies and rules governing the accesses between the clusters in Figure 3.5. We can even control what kinds of actions are allowed for the users on the networking devices, depending on the level of access rights we give them, down to individual commands on the devices.

The most important takeaway from the benefits of software defined networking and access, are the controls we can apply to the network, through the flow we began this chapter with. We can validate the identify and control the level of access all the way to the resource the user would like to access. That is zero trust.

3.4.3.3 VXLAN

VXLAN (Virtual Extensible LAN) and zero trust are two separate but complementary technologies that can be used together to improve network security.

VXLAN is a network virtualization technology that enables the creation of overlay networks over an existing physical network infrastructure. It allows for the segmentation of the network into multiple virtual networks, each with its own security policies and access controls. This segmentation can help to limit the attack surface and reduce the impact of any potential security breaches.

Zero trust, on the other hand, is a security model that assumes no trust, whether inside or outside the network. It is designed to prevent unauthorized access to network resources and data, and to limit the potential damage of any security breaches. Zero trust can help to ensure that all access attempts are authenticated and authorized before granting access to the network.

By combining VXLAN with a zero-trust security model, organizations can improve their overall security posture by reducing the risk of unauthorized access to sensitive data and resources. VXLAN can be used to enforce network segmentation and micro-segmentation policies to limit access to specific resources and data, while zero-trust can ensure that all access attempts are properly authenticated and authorized. This can help to prevent security breaches and limit the impact of any potential breaches that do occur.

3.4.3.4 Application Centric Infrastructure (ACI)

The Cisco ACI (Application Centric Infrastructure) and zero trust are two separate but complementary technologies that can be used together to improve network security.

Cisco ACI is a data center networking solution that provides a centralized policy-based approach to network provisioning and management. It uses a software-defined networking (SDN) model to automate network infrastructure and application services. Cisco ACI can help to simplify network management and reduce complexity, which can improve network security by reducing the risk of human error and misconfiguration.

Zero trust, on the other hand, is a security model that assumes no trust, whether inside or outside the network. It is designed to prevent unauthorized access to network resources and data, and to limit the potential damage of any security breaches. Zero-trust can help to ensure that all access attempts are authenticated and authorized before granting access to the network.

By combining Cisco ACI with a zero-trust security model, organizations can improve their overall security posture by reducing the risk of unauthorized access to sensitive data and resources. Cisco ACI can be used to automate network segmentation and micro-segmentation policies to limit access to specific resources and data, while zero-trust can ensure that all access attempts are properly authenticated and authorized. This can help to prevent security breaches and limit the impact of any potential breaches that do occur.

VXLAN is an integrated component in ACI, as it is used in deploying the technical details of ACI. With ACI we can deploy policies for the individual applications running in ACI, thereby controlling which applications can see and talk with other applications. This way our policies control access and the level of access.

3.5 SD-WAN

Cisco SD-WAN is a software-defined wide-area network technology that can be used to implement a zero-trust security model.

SD-WAN (Software-Defined Wide Area Networking) is a network architecture that enables organizations to manage and optimize network traffic across geographically dispersed locations. SD-WAN can be used to implement a zero-trust network architecture by providing secure connectivity and granular access controls across the network.

One of the key benefits of SD-WAN in the context of zero-trust networking is that it provides secure connectivity across the network, regardless of the location of the user or application. By implementing strong encryption and authentication protocols, SD-WAN can ensure that all network traffic is secure, even when traversing untrusted networks.

SD-WAN can also provide granular access controls that are tied to user identity and context. By integrating with identity and access management systems, SD-WAN can provide dynamic access controls that adapt to user behavior and network conditions, providing a more fine-grained approach to access control.

Another benefit of SD-WAN in the context of zero-trust networking is that it can help reduce the attack surface of the network. By segmenting the network based on user identity and context, administrators can apply more granular access controls and reduce the potential for lateral movement by attackers.

Overall, SD-WAN can be a valuable tool for implementing zero-trust networking, providing secure connectivity, granular access controls, and reduced attack surface. By leveraging the programmability and centralized management capabilities of SD-WAN, administrators can more easily implement a zero-trust architecture and protect against advanced threats.

With SD-WAN, administrators can use software-defined networking (SDN) capabilities to create a network architecture that is optimized for cloud applications and distributed workloads. SD-WAN provides network segmentation and application-aware routing capabilities that allow administrators to define and enforce policies for user and device access. These policies can be based on a user's identity, device type, location, and other contextual factors.

To implement a zero-trust security model with Cisco SD-WAN, administrators can use the following features:

1. Application-aware routing: SD-WAN can dynamically route traffic based on application requirements and network conditions. Administrators can use this feature to create policies that route sensitive traffic through specific paths and apply additional security measures, such as encryption.
2. Security integration: Cisco SD-WAN can be integrated with other Cisco security technologies, such as Cisco Umbrella and Cisco AMP for Endpoints. This integration can provide advanced threat detection and mitigation capabilities that can help to protect against advanced cyber-attacks.
3. Multi-factor authentication: SD-WAN can be configured to require multi-factor authentication (MFA) for user access. MFA can help to reduce the risk of credential theft and improve overall security posture.
4. Continuous monitoring: SD-WAN provides real-time visibility into network traffic, allowing administrators to detect anomalies and potential security threats. This feature can help organizations quickly respond to security incidents and mitigate potential damage.

Cisco SD-WAN provides a set of capabilities that can be used to implement a zero-trust security model. By using SDN to create a dynamic, policy-driven environment, organizations can enforce access policies based on contextual factors and reduce the attack surface of the network. Additionally, the security integration and continuous monitoring capabilities of SD-WAN can help to detect and mitigate potential security threats in real-time.

3.6 TACACS+

TACACS+ (Terminal Access Controller Access-Control System Plus) is a network protocol commonly used for authentication, authorization, and accounting (AAA) in network devices. While TACACS+ itself does not directly align with the principles of zero trust, it can be used as part of a broader zero-trust framework to enhance network security.

- Authentication: TACACS+ provides robust authentication capabilities to verify the identities of users attempting to access network resources. It supports a wide range of authentication methods, including passwords, two-factor authentication (2FA), and digital certificates.
- Authorization: TACACS+ allows for fine-grained authorization control, enabling administrators to define access policies based on user roles, device types, or other contextual factors. This allows for the implementation of the principle of least privilege, ensuring that users have appropriate access rights based on their specific needs.
- Command authorization: TACACS+ can enforce granular command-level authorization, allowing administrators to define which commands or operations a user is permitted to execute on a network device. This helps restrict unauthorized actions and enhances security.
- Accountability and auditing: TACACS+ supports accounting functionality, which enables the logging and auditing of network access events. It generates detailed audit logs that capture user activities, including authentication attempts, authorization decisions, and commands executed. These logs provide visibility into user actions and aid in troubleshooting, compliance, and security incident investigations.
- Centralized management: TACACS+ enables centralized management of authentication, authorization, and accounting policies. It allows administrators to define and maintain these policies from a central server or controller, making it easier to enforce consistent security measures across the network.
- Redundancy and failover: TACACS+ supports redundancy and failover mechanisms to ensure high availability and fault tolerance. It allows for the configuration of multiple TACACS+ servers, ensuring that authentication and authorization services remain operational even in the event of server failures.
- Encryption and security: TACACS+ incorporates encryption to protect the confidentiality and integrity of communication between clients and servers. By using encryption protocols like SSL/TLS, TACACS+ helps secure sensitive authentication information and prevent unauthorized access to credentials.

Personally, I am especially fond of the features in TACAS+ that make it possible to provide granular access to individual commands in Cisco equipment. For some reason I do not see this functionality rolled out that much in actual infrastructures but given the increased importance of the network for a well-functioning business, I expect this to change.

3.7 RADIUS

RADIUS has many of the same features as TACACS+, but without the functions for granular access to individual commands on Cisco equipment. Some of the key features of RADIUS are:

- Authentication: RADIUS provides authentication services by verifying the identities of users attempting to access network resources. It supports a range of authentication methods, including password-based authentication, challenge-response protocols, token-based authentication, and more.

- Authorization: RADIUS allows for centralized authorization management. It provides the ability to define access policies, such as granting or denying access to specific resources or services based on user attributes, network conditions, or other contextual factors. This enables administrators to enforce access controls and implement the principle of least privilege.
- Accounting: RADIUS supports accounting functionality to track and log user activities on the network. It captures information such as login/logout events, session duration, data transfer, and other relevant details. Accounting data can be used for billing purposes, network management, and auditing user behavior.
- Integration with directory services: RADIUS can integrate with various directory services, such as LDAP (Lightweight Directory Access Protocol) or Active Directory, for user authentication and authorization. This integration allows organizations to leverage their existing user databases and centralize user management.
- Scalability: RADIUS is designed to handle large-scale deployments. It supports scalability by enabling the use of distributed RADIUS servers, load balancing techniques, and failover mechanisms. This ensures high availability and performance in environments with a significant number of users or network devices.
- Security: RADIUS incorporates security measures to protect authentication information and communication between clients and servers. It supports encryption protocols such as EAP (Extensible Authentication Protocol) and supports the use of secure transport protocols like SSL/TLS. These security measures help safeguard sensitive user credentials and prevent unauthorized access.
- Interoperability: RADIUS is a widely adopted standard protocol that promotes interoperability among networking equipment and software from different vendors. This enables organizations to implement a unified AAA infrastructure across heterogeneous network environments.

3.8 MFA

Multi-factor authentication might be associated with logging onto an operating system or application, but MFA is equally important at the networking level. Let's begin with access to the networking components. Depending on the level of access the person has to the device, the person can break an entire network by just fiddling with the routing settings on a router. Using MFA before giving access to these devices seems like a smart move. Unfortunately, many of the clients we have are not using MFA for access to networking equipment.

Using MFA, before giving access to a user device, like a laptop, tablet or mobile phone is equally important. How do we know that the device and the users have rights to use the network, without authenticating them? Using MFA as an extra layer of authentication before giving access to a core resource like the network is a zero-trust way of thinking. MFA will be mentioned in the next chapter as well, where we will be looking at the identity part of zero-trust.

3.9 VPN

VPN has been the go-to solution for remote access to the infrastructure for decades now and with zero-trust becoming the new black, VPNs are becoming the solution to the concept of zero-trust network access. But VPNs cannot be seen as the only solution to remote access, we need to apply policies in the same manner as we do for software defined networking and access.

Historically, when you connected to a company network via VPN, you got access to the entirety of the inside, something that a zero-trust way of thinking will find unacceptable. Take a look at Figure 3.6.

Figure 3.6: Zero-trust requires us to think about the level of access as well as how wide that access is for our VPN users.

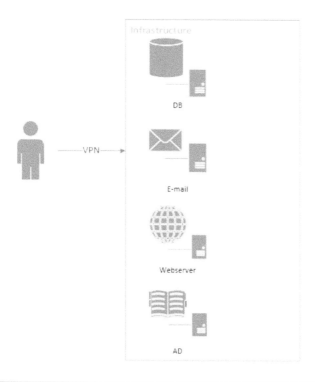

Should a VPN user have access to the entirety of the infrastructure? Maybe, but in most cases the VPN user is logging on for a specific purpose, like access to an ERP system. Why not, then, restrict access to only the ERP system. Using policies to control the access for both VPN users and on-premises users is called zero-trust network access. Beginning a zero-trust journey at the networking layer creates a foundation for all of the additional steps needed to implement a zero-trust architecture for the business or organization.

3.10 Challenges

Apart from some of the migration issues associated with moving from implicit trust to zero trust, there are several other issues security leaders should consider. First, the PE and PA components must be properly configured and maintained. An enterprise administrator with configuration access to the PE's rules might be able to perform unapproved changes or make mistakes that can disrupt operations. A compromised PA could allow access to resources that would otherwise not be approved. These components must be properly configured and monitored, and any changes must be logged and be subject to audit.

Second, because the PA and PEP are making decisions for all access requests to resources, these components are vulnerable to denial-of-service or network disruption attacks. Any disruption to the decision process could adversely affect a company's operations. Policy enforcement can reside in a properly secured cloud environment or replicated in different locations to help lower this threat, but it does not eliminate the threat completely.

Third, stolen credentials and malicious insiders can still do damage to a company's resources. However, a properly developed and implemented zero-trust architecture would limit the damage from such an approach, due to systems being able to figure out who was making the request and whether it was proper. For example, monitoring systems would be able to detect if a janitor's stolen credentials were suddenly trying to access the credit-card number database.

Fourth, security officials need to be sure that adopting a zero-trust strategy does not create a large amount of security fatigue, in which users are constantly being asked for credentials, passwords, and OS patch checks that would eventually affect productivity in a negative way. Here, a balance needs to be struck between the ability of employees and contractors to get their work done and making sure they are not attackers.

Gartner has created a model called Secured Access Service Edge (pronounced "sassy") that combines networking and network security services such as Zero Trust Network Access (ZTNA), software-defined wide area networks (SD-WAN), cloud access security brokers (CASB), Firewall as a Service (FWaaS) and Secure Web Gateways (SWG).

When delivered through a common framework, SASE can provide companies with consistent security and access to several types of cloud applications. This also gives companies a way to simplify their management, maximize network protection across their resources and no matter their location.

While zero trust can be deployed by enterprises that utilize cloud-based services, the SASE model can often provide more guidance through those other technologies.

3.11 Outro

Implementing a zero-trust security model at the networking layer involves creating a network architecture where access to resources is granted based on contextual factors, rather than simply allowing access based on a user's network credentials. This approach can help organizations to reduce the attack surface of their network and better defend against insider and external threats.

There are several key principles of implementing a zero-trust security model at the networking layer:

1. Network segmentation: By dividing the network into smaller, more secure segments, organizations can reduce the attack surface and limit the impact of a potential security breach. Network segmentation can be based on factors such as user groups, device types, and application requirements.
2. Dynamic access control: Access to network resources should be granted based on contextual factors such as user identity, device type, and location, rather than simply allowing access based on a user's network credentials. This approach can help organizations to prevent unauthorized access to network resources.
3. Micro-segmentation: This is a technique where network segmentation is taken to the next level by breaking down the network into smaller segments based on factors such as application requirements and workload types. Each micro-segment can have its own access policies and security controls, which can help to further reduce the attack surface of the network.
4. Multi-factor authentication: By requiring users to authenticate using multiple factors such as a password and a token or biometric authentication, organizations can reduce the risk of credential theft and improve overall security posture.

5. Continuous monitoring: Organizations should monitor their network for anomalous behavior and potential security threats in real-time. This can help to detect and respond to security incidents quickly, reducing the potential damage.

Implementing a zero-trust security model at the networking layer involves creating a dynamic, policy-driven environment where access to network resources is granted based on contextual factors. By using techniques such as network segmentation, dynamic access control, and multi-factor authentication, organizations can better defend against insider and external threats while maintaining a strong security posture.

4

Zero Trust Identity

In this chapter we will be using Microsoft Azure AD as the identity provider, for our discussions. This should not be seen as if this option is the only one for a zero-trust identity approach. This is just the vendor with which we are most familiar. Oracle, IBM and SAP, for instance, have their own identity providers that can be used for a zero-trust identity project as easy as Azure AD from Microsoft, or they can choose to use Azure Ad as the identity provider for their own software.

Like before we will be using Figure 4.1 from Chapter 2 as the basis for the identity examples in this chapter:

Figure 4.1: Validation an identity through the entire flow from the upper left to the lower right is the essence of zero-trust.

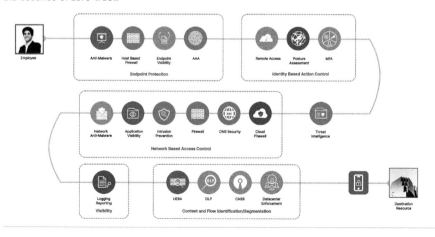

Again, the focus is on getting the person in the upper left corner secure access to the resource in the lower right one, with a focus on the identity part of the process. Not all the steps will be relevant in this chapter, but the AAA, MFA Remote Access and DLP are all relevant for the identity part of a zero-trust project.

The flexibility on the part of Azure AD is a core reason for us choosing this identity platform as the basis for this chapter. Azure AD can integrate with thousands of different applications, as well as be integrated as the identity platform for new application development.

Azure AD can be used as policy engine (PE), policy administrator (PA), and policy enforcement point (PEP). This makes Azure AD the natural choice for all the organizations out there that have based their infrastructure on technologies from Microsoft.

4.1 Identity

Identity has become the core way that organizations can protect themselves and apply policies to as part of their cybersecurity steps. Why? The new way of working, something that was exacerbated with the global Covid pandemic; we are no longer working strictly from within the corporate premises. We are distributed across the world in some cases and working from home in others.

Because of this the traditional ways of securing the enterprise with firewalls and antivirus tools are no longer enough. These tools are still in use of course, but they cannot protect the organization when the users are using their own equipment to access the company resources or the home network, devices and resources that are not under the control of the organization. What to use then?

Identity is the only real way that we can control access to company resources and systems. Identity has been used for this for decades, but the importance of securing and controlling the identities used are of critical importance, not just for zero-trust projects, but for the overall security of businesses and organizations. Look at Figure 4.2 to see how identities are the core control in various IT systems/areas

The importance of identities in cybersecurity in general, and zero trust in particular, all boils down to the following points:

- Verify identities with strong authentication.
- Connect all your users and applications.
- Control access with policies and risk assessments.
- Enforce least privilege access with strong governance.

Figure 4.2: Identity validation from the left to the right, for the devices before they get access to applications, the network and data ensures a zero-trust through the entire flow.

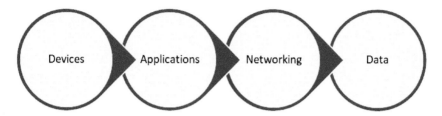

The "connect the users and applications" point deserves a little more detail. We can, in many applications, like SQL Server, Oracle and Cisco equipment, create local users on applications or devices. By making sure that these applications and equipment are connected to the same core identity management system, we avoid the additional overhead of administering identities in multiple places, as well as avoiding the risk of errors on the part of us humans.

Having just one place where we are creating and maintaining users and access rights, and connect other systems/applications to this, decreases the complexity of managing users and user rights. This centralized management of the users provides us with easy management of credentials to applications and systems and organization. See Figure 4.3 for an overview, especially that Azure AD can be used with other cloud providers as well!

4.2 Azure AD

Azure Active Directory (Azure AD) is Microsoft's cloud-based identity and access management service that enables organizations to manage user identities and access to resources, both on-premises and in the cloud. Azure AD supports various authentication methods, including password-based authentication, multi-factor authentication, and conditional access.

One of the key benefits of Azure AD in the context of zero-trust networking is that it provides strong authentication mechanisms that can adapt to changing risk conditions. By implementing multi-factor authentication and conditional access policies, Azure AD can ensure that users are who they claim to be, and that they are only granted access to resources and applications that they are authorized to access.

Azure AD can also provide granular access controls that are tied to user identity and context. By integrating with other security solutions, such as endpoint detection and response (EDR) and security information and event management (SIEM), Azure AD can provide dynamic access controls that adapt to user behavior and network conditions.

Another benefit of Azure AD in the context of zero-trust networking is that it can help reduce the attack surface of the network. By implementing strong access controls and authentication mechanisms, Azure AD can limit the potential for unauthorized access and data breaches.

Overall, Azure AD can be a valuable tool for implementing zero-trust networking, providing strong authentication and access controls, and reducing the attack surface of the network. By integrating with other security solutions and leveraging the scalability and flexibility of the cloud, administrators can more easily implement a zero-trust architecture and protect against advanced threats.

Azure AD provides several features that align with the principles of zero trust. For example, Azure AD supports multi-factor authentication and conditional access, which can help ensure that only authorized users and devices can access resources. Azure AD also provides integration with Azure Security Center, which can help detect and respond to threats in real-time.

In addition, Azure AD provides capabilities for identity and access management for SaaS applications, which can help organizations extend their

Figure 4.3: I have chosen Azure AD as the core identity store because of its flexibility, but you can use AD if that is your core identity management systems as well.

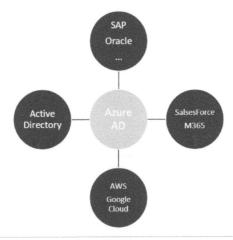

zero trust security policies to cloud-based resources. Azure AD also supports integration with other Microsoft security solutions, such as Microsoft Defender for Endpoint and Microsoft Cloud App Security, which can provide additional layers of protection for enterprise resources.

Let us begin an elaboration on some of the points made above.

4.2.1 Strong authentication

Passwords have been the go-to authentication method for many decades, but passwords are no longer a strong enough option for authentication. Why? If a user falls for an authentic looking phishing mail and provides their username and password to a website, then that is it, our infrastructure will now, most likely, have unwanted users in the infrastructure.

The only real way of mitigating this risk is by asking the users, and especially the privileged users like domain admins, for multi-factor authentication, MFA. MFA can be realized in multiple different ways:

- FIDO2 Key
- Windows Hello
- Biometrics
- Hard Tokens, like an RSA Token
- Microsoft Authenticator.

Azure AD has its own MFA solution that can be integrated into applications using Azure AD for authentication, or Azure AD can be integrated with the above solutions for MFA. With the advent of multiple cloud solutions in a modern hybrid infrastructure, the importance of strong authentication mechanisms cannot be overstated. With our applications spread around cloud solutions the only real object we have any kind of control over is the identity and authentication mechanisms.

Making Azure AD the core authentication mechanism presents its own risks of course, but the tooling that we have with Azure AD makes the reporting and control over the rights of the end users a much more enticing prospective. Microsoft provides additional tooling for securing and managing Azure AD that can mitigate many risks associated with identities, albeit at an additional cost! The next section looks at the tooling we have in Azure AD and the policy engine for authentication policies.

4.3 Azure AD Tooling

Microsoft is actively developing the feature set of Azure AD, so, at the time you are reading this, more features will undoubtedly be present. In addition to this, Microsoft is fond of changing the navigation to the various features on a regular basis, so expect the navigation in this book, to be changed. This section investigates the core areas of Azure AD, areas that will feature predominately in Azure AD in the coming years as well, in my opinion.

4.3.1 Conditional Access

Azure AD's Conditional Access feature is a powerful tool that can help organizations enforce a zero-trust security model. Conditional Access enables organizations to define policies that restrict access to applications and data based on a variety of factors, such as user location, device state, application sensitivity, and risk level.

With Conditional Access, organizations can ensure that only authorized users with secure devices can access sensitive data or applications, while all other users are blocked. This approach aligns with the zero-trust security model, which assumes that no user or device can be trusted until they are authenticated and verified.

For example, an organization might create a Conditional Access policy that blocks access to a sensitive application from devices that are not compliant with the organization's security policies. The policy might also require multi-factor authentication for all access attempts, regardless of device compliance. This would ensure that only authorized users with secure devices and strong authentication can access the application, even if they are accessing it from outside the corporate network.

In addition to Conditional Access, Azure AD offers other features that can help organizations implement a zero-trust security model, such as Identity Protection and Privileged Identity Management. These features can help organizations detect and respond to identity-based threats and can help manage and control access to privileged accounts and resources.

Conditional Access is the policy engine for authentication in Azure AD, not the only one, but the most important of the options. Look at Figure 4.4.

Note the options above with the preview text in parentheses. These are some of the features that Microsoft are working on at the time I am writing this section of the book. Also note the section at the end, where we can monitor the results and effects of the policies we create with conditional access.

Here I would like to spend a few sentences on monitoring regarding zero-trust in general, not just as it relates to conditional access. Monitoring has been part of logging for decades, but only in recent years has logging become part

Figure 4.4: Policies for the users in Azure AD creates the core of zero-trust in Azure AD.

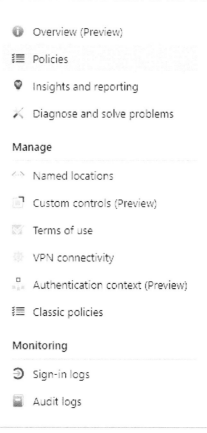

ⓘ Overview (Preview)

▤ Policies

♥ Insights and reporting

✕ Diagnose and solve problems

Manage

⟨⟩ Named locations

▢ Custom controls (Preview)

☑ Terms of use

⚙ VPN connectivity

▢ Authentication context (Preview)

▤ Classic policies

Monitoring

↻ Sign-in logs

▤ Audit logs

of the mainstream of cybersecurity with the advent of SIEM products. If we do not monitor the policies and systems, we are responsible for, how do we know if they are effective? Diligent monitoring also allows us to tune the policies and systems to the reality that the organization faces. Fortunately for us, Azure AD comes with excellent tools for both monitoring and logging.

As I am writing this book, the war in Ukraine is raging back and forth, and cyber-attacks are a core part of the Russian war strategy. Conditional access can be used to create policies where we restrict access to systems using Azure AD as the authentication mechanism from countries in a list. This is where the option called named locations in the Figure 4.4 comes into play. With named locations, we can create policies for things like MFA, based on where the users are coming from, or we can deny access altogether if they are trying to authenticate from a country like Russia. See Figure 4.5 for the named location options.

Figure 4.5: Conditional access in Azure AD gives us the ability to limit access from a subset of countries, or we can use these settings to require additional validation from certain countries around the globe.

+ Countries location + P ranges location ⧉ Configure multifactor authentication trusted IPs

The countries options show a list of countries that we can use as a named location. How does Azure AD know which country the users are coming from? We can configure this setting when we create a named location, see Figure 4.6.

Figure 4.6: Configuring the setting.

None of these options are a guarantee, however. If an attacker is using a VPN connection, the attacker can make it look like they are coming from the country the VPN connection terminates in. Still, using named locations in policies are a way of giving, or denying, access to resources protected by Azure AD.

Conditional Access is an Azure AD tool we can use to apply additional checks based on the location of the users, or we can use the functionality to create a kind of whitelisting for locations under our control, like an HQ, where we will not require the user to use MFA for authentication. Used correctly, conditional access can be the baseline for MFA policies in an organization.

4.4 Identity Governance

Azure AD provides several governance features that can help organizations implement and maintain a zero-trust security model. Here are a few examples:

1. Identity governance: Azure AD offers several identity governance features, such as Access Reviews and Entitlement Management, which can help organizations manage and control access to resources. Access Reviews enables organizations to review and certify the access of users and

groups to various resources, while Entitlement Management provides a centralized approach to manage access to Azure AD-connected applications.

2. Security policy enforcement: Azure AD supports various security policies, such as password policies, conditional access policies, and multi-factor authentication policies, which can help enforce security best practices across the organization.

3. Monitoring and reporting: Azure AD provides several monitoring and reporting features, such as Azure AD sign-in logs, audit logs, and activity logs, which can help organizations detect and respond to security incidents and policy violations.

4. Integration with other security solutions: Azure AD can be integrated with other Microsoft security solutions, such as Microsoft Cloud App Security, Microsoft Defender for Endpoint, and Microsoft Information Protection, which can help organizations extend their zero-trust security model to other areas of their environment.

By leveraging these governance features, organizations can maintain a consistent and controlled approach to access management, ensuring that only authorized users and devices can access resources, and that all access attempts are monitored and audited. This approach aligns with the zero-trust security model, which requires continuous verification of all access attempts, and can help organizations reduce the risk of data breaches and security incidents.

In all, Azure AD comes with a strong set of tools that can help us create governance strictures surrounding our use of Azure AD as an identity source. Having good governance in place in general is good business practice, but it is especially important for good cybersecurity. Here I will focus on governance surrounding identity. See Figure 4.7.

Figure 4.7: Regular review of the users in an application and the level of their rights, ensures that we can continually rely on Azure AD as an updated and trusted identity store.

External user lifecycle   Group membership   Role assignments   Auditing and reporting

This figure is taken from the identity governance section for Azure AD. There are different governance tools in place, depending on the area of identity in question. Here I will focus on the first option, External user lifecycle and the last option, auditing, and reporting. Establishing strong processes and governance around granting access to internal systems, to external users, must be a priority in any organization, not just for zero-trust, but for the overall security of the organization in general.

Having a process in place that does basic hygiene for both Azure AD and the on-prem AD, that removes or makes accounts inactive, is critical to the

Figure 4.8: Process for user rights.

Onboard external users through an approval process

Create a self-service onboarding experience for external users. You can define what access is granted to these users by default, as well as those who need to approve them. Learn more ☐

Create access package

Create access reviews of all guests in Teams and groups

Set up periodic reviews for all guest user access in any Team or group. Reviewers can be a Teams or group owner, a specific set of people, or a guest user themselves. Access that's not approved can be automatically removed. Learn more ☐

Create access review

Review and remove guests with unnecessary access

Set up reviews to remove guest users when they no longer need to collaborate with your organization. Learn more ☐

Create access review

---

security of the authentication system, not just for Azure AD or AD, but for any authentication system.

Unfortunately, this basic hygiene is often not in place! There can be many reasons for this, like service accounts not removed after an application has been retired, or not having a process in place with HR when staff resign or are replaced a different place in the organization, still retaining their user rights from their previous responsibilities (Figure 4.8). Something I see with many customers, unfortunately.

The importance of the security and health of any identity system is becoming increasingly important with the advent of cloud solutions for many applications, like Salesforce for instance. We are now sharing our identities outside of our organizations. This makes the identity system a critical component in the overall security of the organization. Thus, the importance of the health and hygiene of the system.

4.5 Authentication Strength

The strength of authentication is a crucial aspect of a zero-trust security model. Zero-trust assumes that no user or device should be trusted by default, so strong authentication is essential to ensure that only authorized users and devices are granted access to network resources and data.

Strong authentication can be achieved using multi-factor authentication (MFA), which requires users to provide two or more forms of authentication before accessing network resources. This can include something the user knows (such as a password), something the user has (such as a smart card or token), or something the user is (such as a biometric factor like fingerprint or facial recognition).

By implementing strong authentication as part of a zero-trust security model, organizations can significantly reduce the risk of unauthorized access to sensitive data and resources. Even if a user's credentials are compromised, the attacker will not be able to gain access without the additional authentication factor(s). This can help to prevent security breaches and limit the impact of any potential breaches that do occur.

In this chapter we look at the options for controlling and managing the authentication strength of Azure AD. At the time of writing, this functionality is still in preview, but I see the option for us to control this part of Azure AD as a huge benefit to the overall security of authentication, especially when we integrate Azure AD as the authentication system in different application, not necessarily from Microsoft, like SAP or Oracle.

Look at Figure 4.9.

These are some of the options in place as I write this book, more might be added, or removed, when this functionality is out of the preview phase. Note the number of different methods of authentication in the list. The ones you should stay away from are the ones mentioning SMS. SMS has been broken as a second

Figure 4.9: At the point of writing these are the options for MFA with Azure AD, undoubtedly there are more now. MFA is core to the conditional access policies and zero-trust.

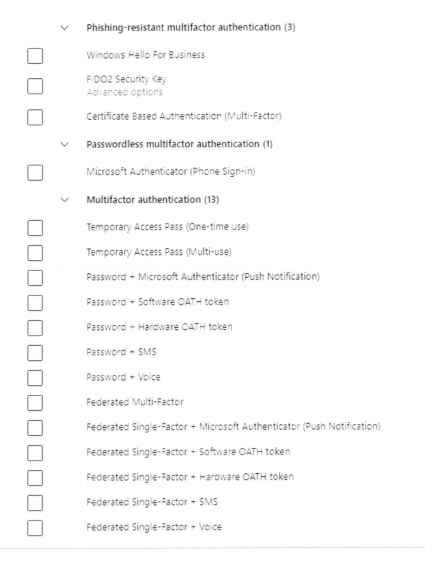

factor for authentication for years and you should expect those to be removed from the list before the preview phase is over.

The temptation might be to choose the strongest in the list, but we need to consider the applications that we are integrating with Azure AD.

Can they handle this kind of authentication? This makes choosing the right authentication method a challenge for many organizations, since they might not be fully aware of the limitations of the applications in their infrastructure. On top of that, some of the applications might be too old to integrate with Azure AD.

This brings us to the core of the challenges of authentication, as it applies to zero trust. I mentioned in Chapter 2, about how to zero trust, that a full assessment of the software and hardware present in the infrastructure and the maintenance level of those must be done before embarking on a zero-trust journey. Apart from giving us a baseline from which to begin the journey, it also provides us with insight into the abilities of the applications for integration into Azure AD. Can that be done, or do we have to restrict ourselves to the on-prem AD?

Not that there is anything wrong with using AD, but a zero-trust project should also use the opportunity to limit the number of authentication systems as part of the project, if possible. Multiple authentication systems possibly mean multiple places of user maintenance, increasing the options of human errors, the ever-present source of mistakes.

4.6 Privileged Identity Management

Privileged identity management (PIM) is a feature of Azure AD that can help organizations implement a zero-trust security model by providing just-in-time access to privileged accounts and roles. PIM enables organizations to control and manage privileged access by creating time-bound assignments for privileged roles and requiring users to request and justify access before being granted it.

PIM can help organizations reduce the risk of privileged access misuse or abuse, by ensuring that users only have access to privileged roles when needed, and that the access is strictly monitored and audited.

Here are a few examples of how PIM aligns with the zero-trust security model:

1. Just-in-time access: PIM provides time-bound access to privileged roles, which means that users only have access to those roles for a specific amount of time. This approach aligns with the zero-trust security model, which requires continuous verification of all access attempts, and can help prevent unauthorized access to sensitive resources.

2. Access reviews: PIM enables organizations to review and certify the access of users to privileged roles, ensuring that only authorized users can access those roles. This aligns with the zero-trust

security model, which assumes that no user or device can be trusted until they are authenticated and verified.

3. Approval workflows: PIM requires users to request access to privileged roles and provides approval workflows to ensure that access requests are reviewed and approved by the appropriate individuals. This approach aligns with the zero-trust security model, which requires continuous monitoring and verification of all access attempts.

Overall, PIM can play a crucial role in implementing a zero-trust security model by providing a controlled and audited approach to managing privileged access. By leveraging PIM, organizations can reduce the risk of privileged access misuse or abuse and ensure that only authorized users with verified identities and devices can access sensitive resources.

A privileged account might not only be the ones built into Azure AD or AD, but a privileged account can also be an application specific account on an ERP system or database.

In Section 4.2.1 on MFA, I mentioned that using MFA for accounts with a high level of sensitive privileges was a must. That is still true but having strong monitoring and logging in place for these kinds of accounts are just as important. Any hacker that compromises a user account will immediately try to elevate that access to a more privileged account. This makes monitoring of these accounts of the utmost importance. Look at Figure 4.10.

Figure 4.10: Formal approval of elevated rights for any length of time is critical for zero-trust.

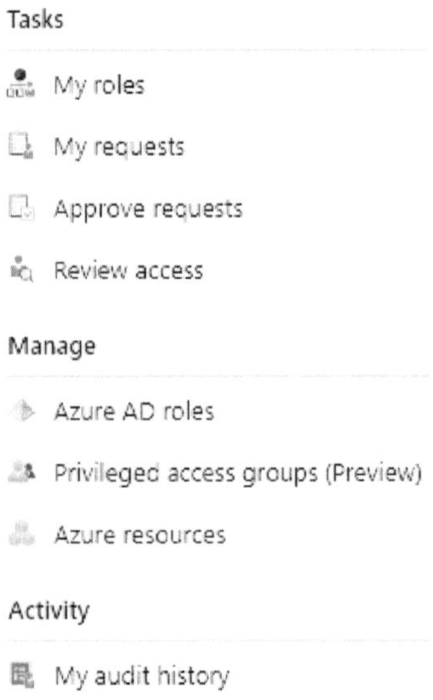

Tasks

👤 My roles

🗔 My requests

🗔 Approve requests

🔍 Review access

Manage

▷ Azure AD roles

👥 Privileged access groups (Preview)

👥 Azure resources

Activity

🗒 My audit history

Note the options My requests and Approve requests. These options make it possible for a privileged role to be requested as well as for this request to be sent to another role for approval. In this way, we can control who gets access to a privileged role by having a flow in place for approval before the role gets assigned to the requestor. Unfortunately, for now this functionality is limited, so we will still need a formal IAM system for these requests to be expanded beyond Azure AD roles.

The auditing in Azure AD for privileged roles is very good, see Figure 4.11.

Figure 4.11: The systems, or application, owners should approve any elevated access rights to their systems or applications.

Approve requests

▷ Azure AD roles

▲ Privileged access groups (Preview)

Azure resources

Azure managed applications

Azure AD provides logging and monitoring for both the roles assigned, as well as the resources that the roles have been accessing while being issued with the privileged role. The last option, called Azure Managed applications, are related to resources that are integrated into Azure AD, thereby extending the logging and monitoring to applications that are not necessarily Azure native in nature.

4.7 IAM

Identity and access management (IAM) is the process of managing user identities and their access to resources and services within an organization. IAM can be used to implement a zero-trust network architecture by providing strong authentication and access controls that are tied to user identity and context.

One of the key benefits of IAM in the context of zero-trust networking is that it provides strong authentication mechanisms that can adapt to changing risk conditions. By implementing multi-factor authentication and conditional access policies, IAM can ensure that users are who they claim to be, and that they are only granted access to resources and applications that they are authorized to access.

IAM can also provide granular access controls that are tied to user identity and context. By integrating with other security solutions, such as endpoint detection and response (EDR), and security information and event management (SIEM), IAM can provide dynamic access controls that adapt to user behavior and network conditions.

Another benefit of IAM in the context of zero-trust networking is that it can help reduce the attack surface of the network. By implementing strong access controls and authentication mechanisms, IAM can limit the potential for unauthorized access and data breaches.

Overall, IAM can be a valuable tool for implementing zero-trust networking, providing strong authentication and access controls, and reducing the attack surface of the network. By integrating with other security solutions and leveraging the scalability and flexibility of IAM systems, administrators can more easily implement a zero-trust architecture and protect against advanced threats.

The Microsoft solution to IAM is not that strong currently, but there are many vendors out there with solutions that can integrate with Azure AD, as well as the identity solutions from the other cloud vendors, like AWS, Google or Oracle cloud infrastructure.

4.8 Outro

Azure AD can help organizations implement a zero-trust security model by providing a comprehensive set of identity and access management capabilities. Here are some examples of how Azure AD aligns with the zero-trust security model.

1. Multi-factor authentication (MFA): Azure AD provides MFA capabilities that can help prevent unauthorized access to resources, by requiring additional forms of authentication beyond the user's password. MFA can help reduce the risk of credential theft or misuse, which is a common attack vector in today's threat landscape.

2. Conditional access: Azure AD's Conditional Access feature enables organizations to define policies that restrict access to resources based on various factors, such as user location, device state, application sensitivity, and risk level. Conditional access policies can help ensure that only authorized users with secure devices can access sensitive data or applications, while all other users are blocked.

3. Identity protection: Azure AD's Identity Protection feature can help organizations detect and respond to identity-based threats, such as suspicious sign-in activity, risky user behavior, or compromised credentials. Identity protection can help organizations reduce the risk of data breaches or security incidents, by providing real-time risk assessments and automated remediation.

4. Azure AD privileged identity management (PIM): As I mentioned earlier, PIM can help organizations manage and control access to privileged accounts and roles, by providing just-in-time access and approval workflows. PIM can help reduce the risk of privileged access misuse or abuse and ensure that only authorized users with a verified need can access sensitive resources.

5. Security monitoring and reporting: Azure AD provides several monitoring and reporting features, such as sign-in and audit logs, that can help organizations detect and respond to security incidents and policy violations. Security monitoring can help organizations maintain a continuous and controlled approach to access management and ensure that all access attempts are audited and verified.

Azure AD provides a powerful set of tools and features we can use to implement and maintain a zero-trust security model. By leveraging Azure AD's capabilities, organizations can ensure that all access attempts are continuously verified and authenticated, and that sensitive resources are only accessible to authorized users with verified identities and devices. This approach can help organizations reduce the risk of data breaches, security incidents, and other cyber threats.

5

Cloud and Zero-trust

Cloud computing can be a valuable tool for implementing a zero-trust network architecture, providing flexibility, scalability, and robust security features.

One of the key benefits of cloud computing in the context of zero-trust networking is that it provides a centralized platform for implementing and managing security controls and policies. By leveraging cloud-based security solutions, administrators can more easily implement and manage access controls, authentication mechanisms, and other security features.

Cloud computing can also provide a more dynamic and flexible approach to zero-trust networking, allowing administrators to easily scale resources and services up or down as needed. This can help organizations respond more quickly to changing threat conditions and adapt their security posture accordingly.

Another benefit of cloud computing in the context of zero-trust networking is that it can provide greater visibility into network activity, enabling administrators to quickly identify and respond to security incidents. By leveraging cloud-based security solutions, administrators can gain real-time insights into network traffic, user behavior, and other key security indicators.

Overall, cloud computing can be a valuable tool for implementing a zero-trust network architecture, providing centralized management, flexibility, scalability, and enhanced security features. By leveraging the benefits of cloud computing, organizations can more easily implement a zero-trust architecture and protect against advanced threats.

5.1 Cloud History

Cloud computing has a relatively recent history that can be traced back to the early 2000s. Here is an overview of the key milestones and developments in the history of cloud computing:

Conceptual origins (1950s–1990s):

- The idea of remotely accessing and utilizing computing power can be traced back to the 1950s and 1960s when mainframe computers were first introduced.
- The concept of time-sharing emerged in the 1960s, enabling multiple users to access a single computer simultaneously.
- The advent of the internet in the 1990s set the stage for the development of cloud computing by providing a global network infrastructure.

Salesforce.com (1999):

- Salesforce.com, founded by Marc Benioff in 1999, pioneered the concept of delivering enterprise applications over the internet.
- It introduced the software-as-a-service (SaaS) model, where software applications are accessed through a web browser rather than being installed on individual computers.

Amazon Web Services (AWS) (2002-2006):

- Amazon Web Services (AWS), launched by Amazon.com in 2002, offered a suite of cloud computing services, including storage, computation, and even human intelligence through the Mechanical Turk service.
- In 2006, AWS introduced the Elastic Compute Cloud (EC2) and the Simple Storage Service (S3), which allowed businesses to rent virtual servers and store data in the cloud.

Google Apps (2006):

- Google launched Google Apps, a suite of productivity and collaboration tools, including Gmail, Google Docs, and Google Calendar.
- This marked Google's entry into the cloud computing market and introduced the concept of web-based productivity applications.

OpenStack (2010):

- OpenStack, an open-source cloud computing platform, was launched in 2010.
- It provided a framework for building and managing private and public clouds, allowing organizations to create their own cloud infrastructure.

Microsoft Azure (2010):

- Microsoft introduced Azure, its cloud computing platform, in 2010.
- Azure provides a range of services, including virtual machines, storage, and developer tools, enabling businesses to build, deploy, and manage applications in the cloud.

Cloud service providers (2010s):

- Over the course of the 2010s, numerous cloud service providers emerged, including Google Cloud Platform (GCP), IBM Cloud, Oracle Cloud, and Alibaba Cloud, among others.
- These providers offered a wide array of services, including infrastructure-as-a-service (IaaS), platform-as-a-service (PaaS), and various software services.

Advancements and adoption (2010s–present):

- Throughout the 2010s and beyond, cloud computing experienced rapid growth and adoption across various industries and organizations.
- The introduction of serverless computing, containerization technologies like Docker and Kubernetes, and advancements in artificial intelligence and machine learning further expanded the capabilities and applications of cloud computing.

5.2 The Future of Cloud

There is a saying that predicting the future is flawed and often wrong; however, I am still going to give it a shot here. Please keep in mind that these are my predictions based on my own experiences and client requests over the past few years.

- Hybrid and multi-cloud adoption: Many organizations will continue to adopt a hybrid cloud approach, combining public and private clouds to leverage the benefits of both. Additionally, multi-cloud strategies will become more prevalent, where businesses utilize multiple cloud providers for different purposes, such as leveraging specific services or avoiding vendor lock-in.
- Edge computing and fog computing: The rise of Internet of Things (IoT) devices and the need for low-latency processing will drive the growth of edge computing and fog computing. Cloud services will extend their reach to the edge of the network, enabling real-time data processing and analysis closer to the source of data generation.
- Serverless computing: Serverless computing, where cloud providers manage the infrastructure and automatically scale resources, will continue to gain popularity. It offers improved resource utilization, reduced operational overhead, and enables developers to focus more on code and functionality rather than infrastructure management.
- Artificial intelligence and machine learning: Cloud platforms will increasingly offer AI and machine learning services, allowing businesses to leverage advanced analytics, natural language processing, computer vision, and predictive modeling capabilities without requiring specialized expertise. These services will be integrated into various applications, making AI more accessible to a wider range of organizations.
- Security and privacy enhancements: As cloud technology matures, there will be a heightened focus on security and privacy. Cloud providers will invest in advanced security measures, such as encryption, threat detection, and identity management, to protect data and ensure compliance

with regulations. Privacy concerns, especially related to data handling and user consent, will continue to be addressed and regulated.

- Quantum computing in the cloud: While still in its early stages, quantum computing has the potential to revolutionize various industries. In the future, cloud providers may offer quantum computing resources and services, allowing organizations to access and experiment with quantum algorithms and applications without needing to build their own infrastructure.
- Green cloud computing: Environmental sustainability will play a significant role in the future of cloud technology. Cloud providers will focus on reducing energy consumption, adopting renewable energy sources, and implementing more efficient data center designs. Additionally, organizations will prioritize cloud providers with strong environmental credentials to align with their sustainability goals.
- Enhanced collaboration and communication: Cloud-based collaboration and communication tools will continue to evolve, offering improved integration, real-time collaboration features, and seamless workflows across different devices and platforms. These tools will enable remote teams to work together effectively and facilitate virtual meetings, file sharing, and project management.
- Cloud integrations. As the customers are beginning to utilize different cloud vendors for different purposes, we will see an increase in integrations between the different cloud vendors. Microsoft and Oracle have already begun integrating the various offerings in their respective clouds with one another, I see this trend increasing in the coming years.

5.3 Zero-trust and Cloud Security

There are very few differences between the zero-trust steps needed in the cloud and those needed in on-prem environments. Take a look at the points below:

- Identity and access management (IAM): Implementing robust IAM practices is crucial for zero trust in the cloud. This involves establishing strong user authentication mechanisms, such as multi-factor authentication (MFA), and implementing fine-grained access controls based on user roles, permissions, and contextual factors.
- Micro segmentation: Cloud environments often consist of multiple interconnected components, such as virtual machines, containers, and services. Micro segmentation involves dividing these components into smaller, isolated segments and enforcing strict access controls between them. This limits lateral movement within the network and reduces the impact of a potential security breach.
- Least privilege: Following the principle of least privilege is fundamental in a zero-trust environment. Users and systems should only have access to the resources and data they explicitly require to perform their tasks. By minimizing unnecessary access rights, the attack surface is reduced, and the potential damage of a compromised user or system is mitigated.
- Continuous monitoring and analytics: Zero trust requires continuous monitoring of user behavior, network traffic, and system activity. Utilizing advanced analytics and machine learning techniques, organizations can identify anomalous behavior and potential threats in real time.

This allows for proactive threat detection and response, helping to prevent or minimize security incidents.

- Encryption and data protection: Protecting data at rest and in transit is a critical component of zero trust in the cloud. Employing strong encryption mechanisms, both for data stored in the cloud and data transferred between different cloud services, ensures that even if an attacker gains access to the data, it remains unreadable and unusable.

- Security automation and orchestration: Cloud environments are highly dynamic, with resources being provisioned, scaled, and decommissioned rapidly. To maintain zero-trust principles, it's important to automate security processes, such as access provisioning, threat detection, and incident response. Security orchestration tools can help streamline these processes and ensure consistent enforcement of security policies.

- Secure remote access: Zero-trust principles are particularly relevant in remote work scenarios, were employees access cloud resources from various locations and devices. Implementing secure remote access solutions, such as virtual private networks (VPNs) or secure access service edge (SASE) architectures, ensures that user connections are authenticated and encrypted, regardless of their location.

If you remember back to some of the earlier chapters, then you will recognize many of the above steps from there. Are there differences between zero trust in on-prem environments and the cloud? Yes, there are, for instance, many cloud vendors that offer SaaS solutions to their customers. In Microsoft Azure for instance there is the Azure SQL offering where customers can use a database in Azure for their data storage needs.

In addition to Azure SQL there are serverless in the mix of SaaS services, all of which need to be implemented in different environments and application scenarios. So, although many of the steps are similar, there are technologies in the cloud that need additional thought before they become zero-trust enabled.

5.3.1 Azure SQL

Azure SQL, the cloud-based database service offered by Microsoft Azure, can be integrated with zero-trust principles to enhance the security of data stored in Azure SQL databases. Here are some key considerations for implementing zero trust with Azure SQL:

- Identity and access management (IAM): Implement strong authentication mechanisms for accessing Azure SQL databases, such as Azure Active Directory (Azure AD) authentication. Azure AD integrates with zero trust principles by providing identity-based access controls and allowing organizations to enforce multi-factor authentication (MFA) for user access.

- Role-based access control (RBAC): Utilize RBAC to assign granular permissions to users or groups accessing Azure SQL. With RBAC, you can follow the principle of least privilege and provide users with only the necessary permissions to perform their tasks within the database.
- Private endpoint: Azure private endpoint enables you to access Azure SQL databases over a private network connection, eliminating the need to expose your database to the public internet. By leveraging private endpoint, you can enforce zero trust principles by ensuring that access to your Azure SQL database is only possible through a private and secure network connection.
- Network security: Implement network security controls, such as Azure Virtual Network (VNet) service endpoints and Azure Firewall, to restrict inbound and outbound traffic to your Azure SQL database. By configuring secure network connections and using firewall rules to allow only authorized traffic, you can reduce the attack surface and enforce zero-trust principles.
- Auditing and monitoring: Enable auditing and monitoring features in Azure SQL to track and log database activities. By leveraging Azure Monitor and Azure Sentinel, you can continuously monitor database access, detect anomalous behavior, and respond to potential security incidents in real time, aligning with zero trust's continuous monitoring principle.
- Encryption: Protect data at rest and in transit by utilizing encryption features provided by Azure SQL. Enable transparent data encryption (TDE) to encrypt data at rest within the database. Additionally, enforce SSL/TLS encryption for data transmission between client applications and Azure SQL to secure data in transit.
- Threat detection and advanced security: Utilize Azure SQL's built-in threat detection capabilities, such as Azure SQL Database advanced threat protection, which employs machine learning algorithms to identify suspicious activities and potential security threats. These features align with zero-trust principles by proactively detecting and responding to potential security risks.
- Data masking and row-level security: Implement data masking and row-level security in Azure SQL to ensure that sensitive data is protected, and access is limited based on defined security policies. Data masking can help obfuscate sensitive data from non-privileged users, while row-level security can restrict data access based on specific conditions or user attributes.

Note that micro segmentation is not in the above list. Micro segmentation needs to be done outside of the Azure SQL service, likewise for monitoring.

5.3.2 Serverless

Azure Serverless, which includes services like Azure Functions and Logic Apps, can be integrated with zero-trust principles to enhance the security of serverless applications and workflows. Here are some considerations for implementing zero trust with Azure Serverless:

- Authentication and authorization: Implement strong authentication mechanisms for accessing serverless functions and workflows. Azure Active Directory (Azure AD) authentication can be used to enforce identity-based access controls and enable multi-factor authentication (MFA) for user access to serverless resources.

- Role-based access control (RBAC): Utilize RBAC to assign granular permissions to users or groups accessing Azure Serverless resources. By following the principle of least privilege, you can provide users with only the necessary permissions to execute and manage serverless functions or workflows.
- Secure inputs and outputs: Apply input validation and output encoding to protect against potential security vulnerabilities, such as injection attacks or cross-site scripting (XSS). Implementing proper validation and encoding techniques ensures that data inputs and outputs in serverless applications are treated securely.
- Encryption and secure communication: Ensure that data at rest and in transit within serverless applications is appropriately encrypted. Azure Key Vault can be used to store and manage encryption keys, and SSL/TLS should be enforced for secure communication between serverless components and external systems.
- Logging and monitoring: Enable logging and monitoring features in Azure Serverless services to track and analyze application activities. Utilize Azure Monitor, Azure Application Insights, or third-party logging solutions to gain visibility into the execution and behavior of serverless functions and workflows. This helps in detecting any suspicious activities or potential security incidents.
- Continuous deployment and security testing: Implement continuous integration and continuous deployment (CI/CD) pipelines for serverless applications, including security testing as part of the pipeline. Incorporate automated security scans and code analysis tools to identify vulnerabilities or misconfigurations during the development and deployment stages.
- Secure storage and secrets management: Use Azure Storage services with appropriate access controls and encryption for securely storing any sensitive data or configuration information needed by serverless functions. Azure Key Vault can be used for secure management of secrets, such as connection strings or API keys, required by serverless applications.
- Regular patching and updates: Keep serverless platforms and dependencies up to date with the latest security patches and updates. Regularly review and apply security patches to ensure that known vulnerabilities are addressed, reducing the risk of exploitation.

Typically, Azure functions, or Azure logic apps, are integrated into larger applications, making the security of these individual components an integral part of the security of the larger application. DevSecOps makes a lot of sense in scenarios where a larger application is composed of smaller self-contained components, like Azure functions or an application that is containerized.

5.4 Hybrid Cloud and Zero Trust

While hybrid cloud environments offer numerous benefits, there are also some risks and challenges associated with their implementation. Here are some common risks of hybrid clouds:

- Data security: Hybrid cloud environments involve the sharing and movement of data between on-premises infrastructure and public cloud services. This introduces the risk of data breaches, unauthorized access, or data leakage during data transfers or while data is at rest in different environments. It is crucial to ensure robust encryption, access controls, and security measures to protect sensitive data.
- Compliance and regulatory challenges: Hybrid cloud deployments may span multiple jurisdictions, each with its own set of regulations and compliance requirements. Managing compliance across different environments can be complex and challenging. Organizations need to ensure they understand and adhere to the relevant compliance frameworks, industry standards, and data protection regulations applicable to their data and operations.
- Complexity and integration: Hybrid cloud environments often involve integrating various technologies, platforms, and services from multiple vendors. This complexity can lead to interoperability issues, configuration challenges, and increased management overhead. Organizations must carefully plan and design their hybrid cloud architecture, considering integration requirements, data flows, and compatibility between different components.
- Dependency on network connectivity: Hybrid cloud environments heavily rely on network connectivity between on-premises infrastructure and cloud services. Any disruptions or latency in the network can impact application performance, availability, and data transfers. Organizations need to ensure reliable network connectivity and have contingency plans in place to handle potential network failures or slowdowns.
- Vendor lock-in: Depending on the specific services and platforms used in a hybrid cloud environment, organizations may face the risk of vendor lock-in. Vendor lock-in occurs when proprietary technologies, APIs, or data formats make it difficult to switch cloud providers or migrate applications and data to another environment. It is important to carefully evaluate the compatibility and portability of services and data between different cloud platforms to mitigate this risk.
- Increased complexity in governance and management: Managing and governing hybrid cloud environments can be more complex compared to traditional IT infrastructure or a single cloud environment. Organizations need to establish clear policies, controls, and monitoring mechanisms to ensure consistent governance, security, compliance, and performance across the hybrid environment. This may require additional resources, specialized skills, and robust management tools.
- Cost management: Hybrid cloud environments can introduce challenges in managing and optimizing costs. Organizations need to carefully monitor and control usage, performance, and resource allocation across the hybrid environment to avoid unexpected cost escalations. Cost visibility, budgeting, and optimization practices are essential to ensure that the economic benefits of the hybrid cloud are realized.

Addressing these risks requires a comprehensive strategy that includes robust security measures, adherence to compliance requirements, careful planning and architecture design, effective governance, and continuous monitoring and optimization. Organizations should conduct thorough risk assessments and work closely with cloud providers and experienced consultants to mitigate the risks associated with hybrid cloud environments.

You might ask yourself why companies and organizations are using multiple clouds when these risks are present? Even if the various cloud vendors slowly integrate their various offerings with each other, limiting some of the above risks, should the companies not have thought of that beforehand?

Maybe, but the reality of a modern organization is that different departments have different needs. Sales might need a strong CRM solution and have chosen Salesforce for that, finance has identified SAP as the solution to their needs and so on, creating the complex realities we see out there in the real world.

See Figure 5.1:

Figure 5.1: Multiple cloud deployments are the reality in many organizations, creating a challenge when trying to implement zero-trust in application distributed across multiple clouds.

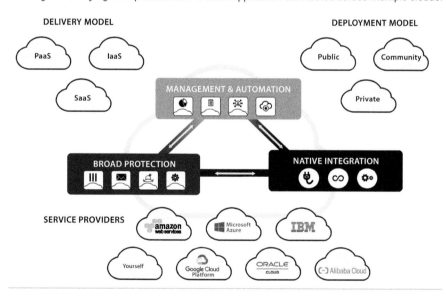

This is the reality in many organizations. Figure 5.2 provides a few more details on the underlying technologies needed to secure a complex cloud setup and integrate it with an on-prem infrastructure.

Hybrid cloud environments can be designed and implemented in alignment with zero-trust principles to enhance security and protect data. Here's how hybrid cloud can integrate with zero trust:

Figure 5.2: Hybrid cloud, lie multi cloud, is a challenge when we are trying to implement zero-trust in applications distributed across local data centres and different cloud vendors.

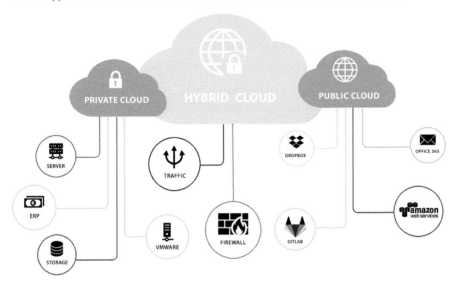

- Identity and access management (IAM): Implement strong authentication mechanisms, such as multi-factor authentication (MFA) and identity-based access controls, across both on-premises and cloud environments. Leverage centralized identity management systems, such as Azure Active Directory (Azure AD), to ensure consistent user authentication and authorization regardless of the location or resource being accessed.
- Network segmentation and micro segmentation: Apply network segmentation principles to separate different segments of the hybrid cloud environment. Use firewalls, virtual private networks (VPNs), and software-defined networking (SDN) solutions to establish secure connections and enforce access controls between segments. Micro segmentation allows for finer-grained access control within each segment, limiting lateral movement and reducing the potential impact of a security breach.
- Encryption and data protection: Employ encryption techniques to protect data at rest and in transit within the hybrid cloud environment. Utilize technologies like transport layer security (TLS) for secure communication between on-premises and cloud components. Implement encryption mechanisms, such as Azure Storage Service Encryption and Azure Disk Encryption, to safeguard data stored in cloud services.
- Zero-trust networking: Adopt zero-trust networking principles in the hybrid cloud environment by implementing solutions such as software-defined perimeter (SDP) or Zero Trust Network Access (ZTNA). These technologies enable granular access controls based on user identity,

device posture, and contextual factors, ensuring that every connection and access request is explicitly verified and authorized.

- Continuous monitoring and analytics: Implement robust monitoring and analytics capabilities to detect anomalies and potential security threats within the hybrid cloud environment. Utilize tools like Azure Security Center, Azure Sentinel, or third-party security information and event management (SIEM) solutions to collect and analyze logs, detect suspicious activities, and enable real-time threat detection and response.
- Security automation and orchestration: Leverage automation and orchestration tools to enforce security policies, manage access controls, and respond to security incidents in a timely manner. Use tools like Azure Policy, Azure Automation, or infrastructure-as-code (IaC) practices to automate the deployment and configuration of security controls across the hybrid cloud environment.
- Regular security assessments and audits: Conduct regular security assessments and audits to identify vulnerabilities, evaluate the effectiveness of security controls, and ensure compliance with industry standards and regulations. Perform penetration testing, vulnerability scanning, and code reviews to identify and remediate potential weaknesses in the hybrid cloud infrastructure.

Integrating zero-trust principles into the design and operation of hybrid cloud environments, organizations can establish a robust security posture that mitigates risks and enhances data protection across both on-premises and cloud environments. It is important to consider the specific needs and characteristics of hybrid cloud deployment and work closely with cloud service providers and security experts to ensure a comprehensive and effective implementation of zero trust.

The "security automation and orchestration" point above is becoming ever more important to cybersecurity. As solutions are becoming ever more complex, we must automate as much of our security posture as possible, especially with the global lack of resources with strong cybersecurity skillsets.

6

5G and Zero-trust

The first question that will enter your mind about a chapter on 5G and mobile networks, is why? Am I right? Well, many vendors, like Cisco from Chapter 3, will allow private organizations and companies to create their own 5G networks, for their own purposes. Industrial infrastructure, like OT from Chapter 5 can benefit from such a private 5G network infrastructure. In this chapter, I will again use Cisco as the example vendor, and again, this is not the only vendor out there that can help you establish a private 5G network infrastructure.

Why has 5G become such an enticing solution from wireless networking for non-mobile service providers? Well, 5G speeds can now compete with the normal wireless standards we are used to from IT infrastructures, like the most recent Wi-Fi 6, although the upcoming standard WI-FI 7 will outpace 5G on speed. A Vodafone cell site with a 5G upgrade is shown in Figure 6.1.

6.1 What is new in 5G?

5G is the next generation of mobile communications technology, after 4G/LTE, being defined for wireless mobile data communication. Radio and Packet Core evolution is being defined to cater to the needs of 5G networks.

Some of the key goals of 5G are:
- Very high throughput (1–20 Gbps).
- Ultra-low latency (<1 ms).
- 1000× bandwidth per unit area.

Figure 6.1: This is a Vodaphone cell tower with 5G implemented.

Source: File:Vodafone 5G Karlsruhe.jpg - https://en.wikipedia.org

- Massive connectivity.
- High availability.
- Dense coverage.
- Low energy consumption.

There are security focused "expert teams" that are a part of many organizations driving 5G architectures. 3GPP and NGMN are two such organizations. This is empowering key 5G security topics into the broader 5G architecture evolution. These topics include authentication, encryption, placement of security controls and sources of visibility. This is all driven by a set of new use cases that drive the 5G architecture.

5G has enabled a new set of possibilities and capabilities. Every new generation of 3GPP wireless mobile data communication technology has set the stage for new set of use cases and capabilities. 3G was the first truly wireless mobile data communication technology that catered to data communication, whereas 4G was the first truly all IP wireless data communication technology. Both 3G and 4G have been instrumental and foundational to the data communication over mobile devices which led to proliferation of applications like video, ecommerce, social networks, games and several other applications on mobile devices. The focus in 3G/4G was more on mobile broadband for consumers and enterprises.

At the same time new sets of use cases are being introduced that are going to throw up new sets of challenges, complexities and threats. The new 5G network will help operators manage current needs as well as gear up for new needs of the upcoming new use cases. 5G is not just going to be about high-speed data connections for enhanced mobile broadband but will enable several new capabilities that can cater to several new enterprise use cases. Securing the "enterprise network slice" presents several new challenges required to securely deliver the outcomes that enterprises that use 5G require, both operationally and by regulatory control. 5G will not just be about serving consumer and enterprise subscribers with high throughput connectivity.

5G will undoubtedly enable new opportunities for operators and companies by being able to cater to requirements for several new enterprise use cases. Cisco envisions 5G to equip operators with more capabilities to cater to enterprise customer needs as well as new use cases. The delivery of these new use cases is predicated on a "safety net" provided by security visibility and controls pervasively throughout the 5G network, from transport all the way up to the applications. 5G provides a few new threat boundaries and, to make it even more difficult, those boundaries are transient, meaning that they can move.

6.2 Why 5G Security?

Security is critical to the success of 5G because it will enable the widespread adoption of this technology by consumers and businesses. 5G networks will offer faster speeds, lower latency, and higher reliability, which will allow for new and innovative use cases, such as autonomous vehicles, remote surgery, and smart cities. However, these benefits will only be realized if the networks are secure.

Here are some of the reasons why security is important to 5G:

- Protecting sensitive data: 5G networks will be used to transmit large amounts of data, including personal information, financial data, and business secrets. Security is essential to protect this sensitive information from being intercepted or stolen by hackers.
- Ensuring network availability: 5G networks will be used to support critical infrastructure, such as healthcare systems, transportation systems, and energy grids. Security is important to ensure that these systems remain available and operational.
- Protecting against cyber-attacks: 5G networks will be more vulnerable to cyber-attacks than previous generations of mobile networks because they will be used to connect a wide range of devices and applications. Security is important to protect against these attacks, which could have serious consequences, such as disrupting critical infrastructure or stealing sensitive data.

- Building trust: 5G networks will only be adopted by consumers and businesses if they trust the networks to be secure. Security is essential to building this trust and ensuring that 5G is widely adopted.
- Meeting regulatory requirements: 5G networks will be subject to strict regulatory requirements, such as those related to data privacy and cybersecurity. Security is important to ensure that these requirements are met and that organizations are not subject to fines or other penalties.

5G security refers to the protection of networks, devices, and data from unauthorized access, attack, or damage in the fifth generation (5G) cellular network. Here is a summary of key points related to 5G security:

1. 5G networks use advanced technologies like virtualization, software-defined networking (SDN), and network slicing to offer high-speed, low-latency connectivity. However, these technologies also introduce new security risks that need to be addressed.
2. Some of the key security risks in 5G networks include attacks on the radio access network (RAN), unauthorized access to network functions, and data breaches. These risks can be mitigated through a combination of technical and procedural measures.
3. 5G networks also introduce new security challenges related to the use of IoT devices, which can be more vulnerable to attack than traditional devices. To address these challenges, security must be built into the design of IoT devices and networks from the outset.
4. The 5G security architecture includes a range of security functions such as encryption, access control, authentication, and network segmentation. These functions work together to protect the network, devices, and data from various security threats.
5. 5G security standards are being developed by various organizations, including the 3rd Generation Partnership Project (3GPP), the International Telecommunication Union (ITU), and the National Institute of Standards and Technology (NIST). Compliance with these standards can help ensure that 5G networks are secure and reliable.
6. To ensure the security of 5G networks, it is important for stakeholders to collaborate and share information about security threats and best practices. This includes network operators, device manufacturers, government agencies, and security researchers.

Point 3 on IoT device security is especially poignant to zero trust, when speaking of 5G security, because of the heterogeneity of the devices that can connect to a 5G infrastructure. 5G touches almost every aspect of the way we live our lives. It's not just about faster, bigger or better, it's about utilizing 5G as an enabler to a series of services that we all will consume in every aspect of our lives.

5G is as much the application of new architectural concepts to traditional mobile networks as it is about the introduction of a new air interface. The 5G mobile network intentionally sets out to be a variable bandwidth heterogeneous access network, as well as a network intended for flexible deployment. Aside from the usual reasons of generational shifts in mobile networks, i.e., those concerned with the introduction of networking technologies on lower cost curves, the 5th generation of mobile networks must be able to allow the mobile service providers to evolve towards new business models that may result in future modes of operation that are very different from those of today. This presents a problem from the viewpoint of securing such a network. The need to be flexible increases the threat surface of the network.

6.3 5G and Critical Infrastructure

5G networks will play a critical role in supporting critical infrastructure. Critical infrastructure refers to systems and assets that are essential for the functioning of society and the economy, including energy grids, transportation systems, healthcare systems, and financial systems. Here are some of the critical infrastructure aspects of 5G:

- Resilience: 5G networks will need to be resilient to disruptions, such as natural disasters or cyber-attacks, in order to support critical infrastructure. This means that the networks will need to be designed with redundancy and failover capabilities to ensure that they remain operational in the event of a disruption.
- Security: 5G networks will need to be secure in order to protect critical infrastructure from cyber-attacks. This includes ensuring that devices and applications that connect to the networks are secure, implementing strong authentication and access control measures, and monitoring the networks for potential security breaches.
- Low latency: 5G networks will offer lower latency than previous generations of mobile networks, which will enable new and innovative use cases for critical infrastructure. For example, 5G networks could be used to support remote surgery or to enable real-time monitoring of energy grids.
- Capacity: 5G networks will need to have the capacity to support the large amounts of data that will be generated by critical infrastructure systems, such as sensors in energy grids or medical devices in healthcare systems.
- Integration: 5G networks will need to be integrated with existing critical infrastructure systems in order to support their operations. This will require collaboration between network operators, infrastructure providers, and government agencies to ensure that the networks are integrated effectively.

These aspects of 5G will only increase as time goes by, and more and more sites get access to 5G communications technology. I will return to the criticality of 5G when we get to the operational technology part of this book.

6.4 Security of Cisco's Private 5G Architecture

Cisco has several security technologies that can be used to secure 5G networks. Here are some examples:

- Cisco Ultra Services Platform: This is a cloud-native platform that provides a secure and scalable architecture for deploying 5G services. It includes built-in security features such as encryption, firewall, and identity and access management.
- Cisco Stealthwatch: This is a network security analytics and visibility solution that can help detect and respond to security threats in real-time. It uses advanced machine learning algorithms to analyze network traffic and identify anomalies.
- Cisco TrustSec: This is a policy-based access control solution that provides secure access to network resources. It uses identity-based policies to ensure that only authorized users and devices can access sensitive data and applications.
- Cisco AnyConnect: This is a secure mobility client that provides VPN access to corporate resources. It can be used to securely connect remote workers and devices to the 5G network.
- Cisco SecureX: This is a cloud-native platform that provides integrated security capabilities across Cisco's security portfolio. It can be used to manage and orchestrate security policies across multiple security products, including those used to secure 5G networks.

There are three main groupings of components in the solution that are relevant to security architecture. These groupings include:

- Enterprise premises: Cisco edge node and radio components are housed on enterprise premises. The edge node hosts packet core components, as well as agents that enable secure connectivity to the cloud. Radio components include remote radio heads as well as centralized and distributed units depending on the model of radio being deployed. Enterprise premises components are responsible for the following capabilities:
  - o Data connectivity from device to the enterprise network
  - o Interface to the radio access network
  - o Interface to the enterprise access network
  - o Access management and session management functionality of the 5G core.

- Cisco Control Center: Housed on Cisco-provided cloud, this is responsible for subscriber management, secure device lifecycle management, and management/operations user interfaces and APIs. Specific capabilities include:
  - o Enterprise ID and policy registered during onboarding, unique Enterprise ID generated to tag all enterprise-related info
  - o Multitenant environment, Enterprise ID used to identify tenancy
  - o Subscriber data – device and SIM info
  - o Authentication credentials
  - o Management access
  - o Key performance indicators (KPIs) and metrics
  - o Usage records
  - o Location information
  - o Deployment configuration data per enterprise.

- Edge orchestration: Offered through Cisco Control Center with functions hosted either on the Cisco private cloud or on the public cloud to expand the geographic footprint of the Control Center. Capabilities that are hosted on public cloud include:
  - Multi-tenant environment, Enterprise ID used to identify tenancy.
  - Management access
  - KPIs and metrics
  - Software images
  - Deployment configuration
  - Configuration backups.

6.5 5G and Zero Trust

Zero-trust security is an approach to security that assumes that all devices, users, and applications are not trustworthy by default, and requires continuous verification and authorization to access network resources. This approach is becoming increasingly important in the context of 5G networks, which are characterized by many connected devices and a high volume of data traffic.

The zero-trust approach to security is particularly relevant in 5G networks because it can help protect against a range of security threats, including attacks on the network infrastructure, data breaches, and unauthorized access to sensitive data and applications.

To implement zero-trust security in 5G networks, organizations need to implement a range of security measures, including:

- Identity and access management: This involves verifying the identity of all devices and users that connect to the network, and controlling their access to network resources based on their identity, role, and context.
- Network segmentation: This involves dividing the network into smaller segments or micro-segments and enforcing access controls between these segments based on policies.
- Threat detection and response: This involves monitoring the network for security threats, and using advanced analytics and machine learning to detect and respond to security incidents in real time.
- Encryption and data protection: This involves encrypting all data traffic that flows over the network and implementing data protection measures such as data loss prevention and data masking to prevent unauthorized access to sensitive data.

Zero trust is an important approach to securing 5G networks and infrastructures, and can help organizations protect against a range of security threats. By implementing a range of security measures such as identity and access management, network segmentation, threat detection and response, and data protection, organizations can create a secure and resilient 5G network that can support their business objectives.

A few more details on the threats that a private 5G infrastructure will bring to the table are in order:

1. Increased attack surface: 5G networks will connect more devices and generate more data than previous networks, which will increase the attack surface for cybercriminals. Zero-trust security can help address this challenge by assuming that all devices and users are untrustworthy by default and verifying their identity and access privileges before allowing them to access network resources.

2. Dynamic network architecture: 5G networks will be more dynamic than previous networks, with the ability to dynamically allocate network resources based on demand. This means that security policies and controls must also be dynamic, and zero-trust security can help ensure that security policies and controls are continually updated to reflect changes in the network.

3. User-centric security: 5G networks will support a range of different devices and user types, including mobile devices, IoT devices, and remote workers. Zero-trust security can help ensure that security policies and controls are user-centric and consider the identity and context of each user and device that accesses the network.

4. Micro-segmentation: 5G networks will support network slicing, which allows multiple virtual networks to be created on a single physical network infrastructure. Zero-trust security can help ensure that each network slice is segmented and isolated from other network slices, and that access controls are enforced between network slices based on policy.

5. Threat detection and response: 5G networks will generate a large volume of data, which can be analyzed using machine learning and other advanced analytics techniques to detect security threats in real-time. Zero-trust security can help ensure that security incidents are detected and responded to in a timely manner, by continuously monitoring the network for security threats and using analytics to identify anomalous behavior.

If you remember back to the chapter on zero-trust at the networking layer of our infrastructures, you will recognize many of the steps from there are repeated here. The technology is different from what we are used to at the networking layer, but the steps to protect are the exact same as for wireless and cabled networking!

In the case of using 5G technology for communications in OT environments, we need to consider a few points:

1. Critical infrastructure: OT systems are used to control and monitor critical infrastructure, such as power plants, water treatment facilities, and transportation systems. These systems are vital to the functioning of society and must be protected from security threats. 5G networks will play an important role in connecting and managing these systems, and therefore must be secured to prevent unauthorized access or attacks.

2. Increased attack surface: The use of 5G networks to connect OT systems will increase the attack surface for cybercriminals. These systems were traditionally designed to be isolated from other

networks, but the use of 5G networks will connect them to a larger ecosystem of devices and networks, creating new vulnerabilities that must be addressed.

3. Compliance and regulations: Many industries that use OT systems are subject to strict compliance requirements and regulations, such as NERC CIP for the electric industry and NIST SP 800-82 for critical infrastructure protection. Failure to secure 5G networks that connect OT systems can result in non-compliance with these regulations, which can result in significant financial penalties and reputational damage.

4. High reliability and availability: OT systems require high reliability and availability to ensure the continuous operation of critical infrastructure. Any security incidents that affect these systems can result in downtime, loss of service, or even physical harm to people or the environment. 5G security must be designed to ensure that security incidents do not affect the availability and reliability of OT systems.

Remember, 5G is a wireless technology and wireless signals propagate, unlike the traditional cabled networking infrastructures. This makes the 5G signals vulnerable to interference from outside parties and malicious attack.

7

Zero-trust Governance/Compliance

Zero-trust compliance is the process of ensuring that an organization's security posture aligns with zero-trust principles and regulatory requirements. Zero-trust compliance involves implementing security controls and processes that are designed to verify the identity and risk posture of users and devices before granting access to network resources. This approach is based on the assumption that any user or device, regardless of its location or previous authentication, could be compromised and therefore must be verified before being granted access to sensitive data or systems.

1. Identity and access management (IAM): IAM is a critical component of zero-trust governance as it ensures that only authorized users and devices have access to network resources. This includes implementing strong authentication methods, such as multi-factor authentication, and regularly monitoring and managing user access to ensure that it remains secure.
2. Network segmentation: Network segmentation involves dividing a network into smaller, isolated sub-networks to limit the spread of any potential security threats. This helps to reduce the attack surface by isolating sensitive data and systems from less secure parts of the network.
3. Real-time monitoring and response: Zero-trust governance requires real-time monitoring and response to detect and respond to security threats as they occur. This involves implementing tools and systems that can detect and respond to security incidents in real-time, such as intrusion detection systems, security information and event management (SIEM) systems, and security orchestration, automation, and response (SOAR) platforms.
4. Data protection: Zero-trust governance places a strong emphasis on protecting sensitive data, such as personal information and financial data. This includes implementing encryption and secure data storage solutions, as well as regularly monitoring and auditing data access to detect and respond to any potential security threats.

5. Application and endpoint security: Zero-trust governance requires that all applications and endpoints, including mobile devices and cloud-based systems, are secured to prevent unauthorized access and data breaches. This includes implementing security solutions such as endpoint protection platforms (EPP) and mobile device management (MDM) solutions.

6. Continuous compliance: Zero-trust governance requires continuous compliance with security and regulatory requirements to ensure that the network remains secure. This involves regularly auditing network security and compliance, as well as updating security policies and procedures to reflect changes in the security landscape.

7. Risk assessment and management: Zero-trust governance requires regular risk assessment and management to identify and address potential security threats. This involves conducting regular security assessments to identify potential vulnerabilities, as well as implementing risk management processes to prioritize and address the most critical security risks.

Like in most of the other chapters, for core guidance on the various steps in governance and compliance for zero-trust is Figure 7.1.

Figure 7.1: Governance extends across the entirety of the infrastructure.

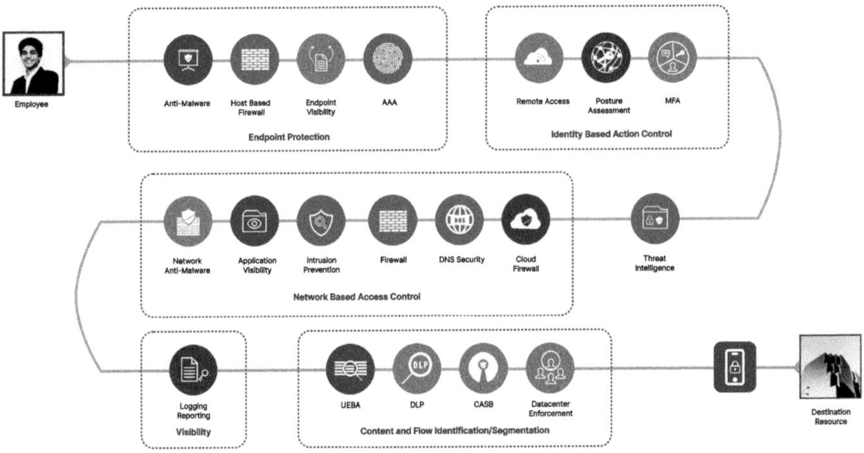

Governance covering the breadth of technologies and processses in a zero-trust implementation is a tall order, but to receive the benefits of zero trust over time, governance that maintains zero trust is a must. If we are to reap the benefits of zero-trust, monitoring of the implementation is of equal importance!

Monitoring in this context is the process of continuously monitoring the activity and behavior of users, devices, and network resources to ensure that they align with an organization's security policies and zero-trust principles. This approach is based on the assumption that any user or device, regardless of its location or previous authentication, could be compromised and therefore must be monitored and verified before being granted access to sensitive data or systems.

Zero-trust monitoring involves implementing tools and systems that provide real-time visibility into the activity and behavior of users, devices, and network resources, and using that information to detect and respond to potential security threats. Some common tools and systems used for zero-trust monitoring include:

1. Security information and event management (SIEM) systems: SIEM systems aggregate and analyze log data from multiple sources, including firewalls, intrusion detection systems, and servers, to provide real-time visibility into network activity and detect potential security threats.
2. Intrusion detection and prevention systems (IDPS): IDPS systems monitor network traffic in real-time and alert administrators to potential security threats, such as malware infections or unauthorized access attempts.
3. Endpoint detection and response (EDR) systems: EDR systems monitor the activity on individual endpoints, such as laptops and mobile devices, to detect and respond to potential security threats, such as malware infections or unauthorized access attempts.
4. Network access control (NAC) systems: NAC systems monitor the activity of devices attempting to connect to the network, and restrict access based on the device's identity, security posture, and network location.
5. User and entity behavior analytics (UEBA) systems: UEBA systems use machine learning algorithms to analyze the activity of users and entities within the network, and detect and respond to potential security threats, such as insider threats or account compromises.

Zero-trust monitoring is a crucial component of a comprehensive security program, as it provides real-time visibility into the activity and behavior of users, devices, and network resources and enables organizations to quickly detect and respond to potential security threats. By implementing a comprehensive set of tools and systems for zero-trust monitoring, organizations can reduce the risk of security incidents and protect sensitive data and systems from potential threats (Figure 7.2).

There is a multitude of different governance frameworks out there. In the following sections I will touch upon the ones I find to be most valuable and important for a modern organization.

Figure 7.2: Governance is core to successfully maintain a zero-trust implementation, as well as cybersecurity in general.

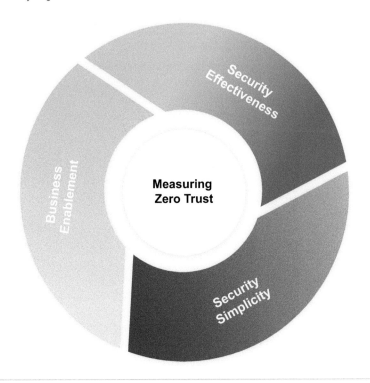

7.1 COBIT 2019

COBIT 2019 is a framework for governance and management of enterprise information and technology (I&T) that can be used in conjunction with a zero-trust security approach. COBIT 2019 provides a comprehensive set of best practices and guidance for I&T governance and management, covering a wide range of areas, including risk management, security, process management, and performance management.

When it comes to security, COBIT 2019 provides guidance on implementing a comprehensive security program, including the development of security policies, the implementation of technical security controls, and the management of security incidents. The COBIT 2019 framework can be used in conjunction with a zero-trust security approach by incorporating zero-trust principles and practices into the overall security program.

For example, COBIT 2019 can be used to guide the implementation of identity and access management (IAM) and real-time monitoring and response, two key components of a zero-trust security program. COBIT 2019 can also be used to support the development and implementation of security policies and procedures that align with zero-trust principles, such as continuously verifying the identity and risk posture of users and devices before granting access to network resources.

COBIT 2019 can be used in conjunction with a zero-trust security approach to provide comprehensive guidance for I&T governance and management, including the development and implementation of a comprehensive security program. By incorporating zero-trust principles and practices into the overall security program, organizations can reduce the risk of security incidents and protect sensitive data.

7.2 IEC/ISO 27001

ISO/IEC 27001 is an international standard for information security management that provides a comprehensive framework for managing and protecting sensitive information. The zero-trust security model can be integrated with ISO/IEC 27001 to provide a robust and comprehensive approach to information security.

In a zero-trust model, access to information and resources is based on the principle of continuous verification, which means that each request for access must be verified and authenticated in real-time before being granted. This approach is in line with the principles of ISO/IEC 27001, which states that access to information should be granted only to those who need it, and that access should be restricted based on the principle of least privilege.

ISO/IEC 27001 provides a comprehensive set of information security controls that can be used in conjunction with a zero-trust security model, including:

1. Access control: ISO/IEC 27001 provides guidance on the implementation of access control policies and procedures, including the use of authentication mechanisms and the implementation of access control systems.
2. Incident management: ISO/IEC 27001 provides guidance on the management of security incidents, including the development of incident response plans and the use of incident management systems.

3. Risk management: ISO/IEC 27001 provides guidance on the management of information security risks, including the identification and assessment of risks, the development of risk mitigation plans, and the implementation of risk management processes.

4. Cryptographic controls: ISO/IEC 27001 provides guidance on the use of cryptographic controls to protect sensitive information, including the use of encryption algorithms and the management of encryption keys.

The zero-trust security model can be integrated with ISO/IEC 27001 to provide a comprehensive approach to information security. By incorporating the principles and practices of the zero-trust security model into the information security management framework provided by ISO/IEC 27001, organizations can reduce the risk of security incidents and protect sensitive information from potential threats.

7.3 SABSA

SABSA (Sherwood Applied Business Security Architecture) is a security framework for enterprise architecture that provides a structured and systematic approach to designing and implementing security solutions. The zero-trust security model can be integrated with SABSA to provide a robust and comprehensive approach to information security.

In a zero-trust model, access to information and resources is based on the principle of continuous verification, which means that each request for access must be verified and authenticated in real-time before being granted. This approach aligns well with the SABSA framework, which emphasizes the need for strong identity and access management controls, including the use of multi-factor authentication and role-based access controls.

SABSA provides a six-layer security architecture that can be used in conjunction with a zero-trust security model, including:

1. Identity and access management: SABSA provides guidance on the implementation of identity and access management controls, including the use of authentication mechanisms and the implementation of access control systems.

2. Network security: SABSA provides guidance on the implementation of network security controls, including the use of firewalls, intrusion detection systems, and virtual private networks (VPNs).

3. Data security: SABSA provides guidance on the implementation of data security controls, including the use of encryption algorithms, data backup and recovery systems, and data loss prevention systems.

4. Application security: SABSA provides guidance on the implementation of application security controls, including the use of secure coding practices, application firewalls, and web application security solutions.
5. Physical security: SABSA provides guidance on the implementation of physical security controls, including the use of access control systems, security cameras, and security alarms.
6. Operations security: SABSA provides guidance on the implementation of operations security controls, including the use of security information and event management (SIEM) systems, intrusion detection and prevention systems (IDPS), and incident response plans.

So, the zero-trust security model can be integrated with the SABSA framework to provide a comprehensive approach to information security. By incorporating the principles and practices of the zero-trust security model into the security architecture provided by SABSA, organizations can implement a comprehensive security architecture and align it with the business needs.

7.4 TOGAF

TOGAF (The Open Group Architecture Framework) is a framework for enterprise architecture that provides a structured and systematic approach to designing, planning, and implementing enterprise architecture. The zero-trust security model can be integrated with TOGAF to provide a robust and comprehensive approach to information security.

In a zero-trust model, access to information and resources is based on the principle of continuous verification, which means that each request for access must be verified and authenticated in real-time before being granted. This approach aligns well with the TOGAF framework, which emphasizes the need for a comprehensive and integrated approach to enterprise architecture, including the implementation of strong identity and access management controls.

TOGAF provides a four-layer architecture framework that can be used in conjunction with a zero-trust security model, including:

1. Business architecture: TOGAF provides guidance on the design of business processes and information systems, including the implementation of business-driven security controls.
2. Data architecture: TOGAF provides guidance on the design of data systems and data management processes, including the implementation of data security controls.
3. Application architecture: TOGAF provides guidance on the design of applications and application systems, including the implementation of application security controls.
4. Technology architecture: TOGAF provides guidance on the design of technology systems and technology infrastructure, including the implementation of network security controls and the use of virtualization and cloud computing technologies.

Like the ones above, the zero-trust security model can be integrated with the TOGAF framework to provide a comprehensive approach to information security. This includes software development efforts, in which TOGAF is a strong framework!

7.5 NIST

NIST (National Institute of Standards and Technology) is a non-regulatory agency of the US Department of Commerce that provides guidance, standards, and best practices for information security and technology. The zero-trust security model aligns well with the NIST framework and its guidance on implementing a risk-based approach to information security.

NIST has published several guidelines and standards that can be used to implement a zero-trust security model, including NIST SP 800-53, NIST SP 800-63, and NIST SP 800-171.

NIST SP 800-53 provides guidance on the implementation of security controls for information systems and organizations, including the implementation of access control mechanisms, network security, and data security controls.

NIST SP 800-63 provides guidance on the implementation of identity and access management controls, including the use of multi-factor authentication, password management, and the implementation of identity management systems.

NIST SP 800-171 provides guidance on the protection of controlled unclassified information (CUI) in non-federal information systems and organizations.

The zero-trust security model aligns well with the NIST framework and its guidance on implementing a risk-based approach to information security. By incorporating the principles and practices of the zero-trust security model into the information security framework provided by NIST, organizations can reduce the risk of security incidents and protect sensitive information from potential threats.

NIST was the first organization that came up with a concrete set of guidance for zero-trust architecture, in the form of the document 800-207, we look at that one next.

7.5.1 NIST 800-207

NIST SP 800-207 is a publication from the National Institute of Standards and Technology (NIST) that provides guidance on the implementation of the zero-trust architecture (ZTA) model. The publication provides an overview of the ZTA model, including its key concepts and principles, and provides guidance on how to design, implement, and operate a zero-trust network.

According to NIST SP 800-207, a zero-trust network is a network architecture that assumes that all entities within the network, including devices, users, and applications, are untrusted until proven otherwise. This approach is based on the principle of continuous verification, which requires that each request for access to information or resources be verified and authenticated in real-time before being granted.

The publication provides guidance on the implementation of ZTA in six key areas, including:

1. Identity and access management: This section provides guidance on the implementation of identity and access management controls, including multi-factor authentication, password management, and the use of identity management systems.
2. Network security: This section provides guidance on the design and implementation of network security controls, including firewalls, intrusion detection systems, and virtual private networks (VPNs).
3. Data security: This section provides guidance on the implementation of data security controls, including data encryption, data loss prevention (DLP), and data backup and recovery.
4. Endpoint security: This section provides guidance on the implementation of endpoint security controls, including antivirus software, endpoint detection and response (EDR) systems, and device management systems.
5. Application security: This section provides guidance on the implementation of application security controls, including web application firewalls (WAFs), application whitelisting, and the implementation of secure software development practices.
6. Incident response: This section provides guidance on the design and implementation of incident response plans, including the creation of incident response teams, the development of incident response procedures, and the use of incident response tools.

NIST SP 800-207 provides comprehensive guidance on the implementation of the zero-trust architecture, and it is an important standard for many financial institutions, because of the international regulation of that industry.

7.6 IEC 62443

IEC 62443 is a comprehensive standard for industrial cybersecurity that provides guidance on how to implement a security program that can protect industrial automation and control systems (IACS) from cyber threats. The standard emphasizes the importance of a zero-trust security model in IACS environments, where the assumption is that no user, device, or network can be trusted until proven otherwise.

To implement a zero-trust security model in an IACS environment, IEC 62443 recommends a set of governance practices that include:

1. Risk assessment: Conduct a comprehensive risk assessment to identify the assets, threats, vulnerabilities, and risks that exist within the IACS environment. The risk assessment should provide a clear understanding of the potential impacts of a cyber-attack, and inform the development of a risk management strategy.
2. Policy development: Develop a set of policies that define the organization's security objectives, requirements, and responsibilities. The policies should be aligned with the organization's overall business goals and should include clear guidance on access control, identity management, data protection, incident response, and other key security topics.
3. Access control: Implement access controls that limit access to IACS resources based on the principle of least privilege. The access controls should be based on a strong authentication mechanism, such as multi-factor authentication, and should be enforced through an identity and access management (IAM) solution.
4. Network segmentation: Implement network segmentation to separate IACS networks and devices based on their function and criticality. Network segmentation can help contain the impact of a cyber-attack and reduce the risk of lateral movement by attackers.
5. Continuous monitoring: Implement a continuous monitoring program to detect and respond to security incidents in real time. The monitoring program should include a set of key performance indicators (KPIs) that provide insight into the effectiveness of the security controls and should be supported by a robust incident response plan.

Overall, IEC 62443 emphasizes the importance of a zero-trust security model in IACS environments and provides guidance on how to implement a governance program that can support this model. By following the recommended governance practices, organizations can reduce the risk of cyber-attacks and ensure the safety, reliability, and availability of their industrial automation and control systems.

7.7 HIPAA

HIPAA (Health Insurance Portability and Accountability Act) is a United States law that establishes standards for the privacy and security of personal health information (PHI). HIPAA applies to covered entities, which include healthcare providers, health plans, and healthcare clearinghouses, as well as their business associates.

Zero trust can be a useful framework for organizations subject to HIPAA regulations. By implementing a zero-trust model, organizations can ensure that only authorized individuals or devices can access PHI, regardless of whether they are within the organization's network or accessing resources remotely. This can help to prevent unauthorized access to PHI, which is a violation of HIPAA regulations.

In addition to implementing a zero-trust model, organizations subject to HIPAA should also take other steps to ensure compliance with the law, such as conducting regular risk assessments, training employees on security policies and procedures, and implementing appropriate technical safeguards, such as encryption and access controls.

7.8 CIS 18

CIS (Center for Internet Security) Controls version 18 is a set of best practices designed to help organizations improve their cybersecurity posture. The CIS Controls provide a prioritized list of cybersecurity actions that organizations can take to reduce their risk of cyber-attacks.

Zero trust can be a useful framework for implementing some of the CIS Controls, such as Control 5, which focuses on limiting access to sensitive data and systems. By implementing a zero-trust model, organizations can ensure that only authorized individuals or devices can access sensitive data and systems, which can help to reduce the risk of cyber-attacks.

In addition to implementing a zero-trust model, organizations can also implement other CIS Controls to improve their cybersecurity posture, such as implementing multifactor authentication (Control 1), securing network devices (Control 11), and monitoring systems for unauthorized access (Control 16). By combining zero trust with other best practices from the CIS Controls, organizations can improve their cybersecurity defenses and better protect their assets from cyber threats.

7.9 Cloud Security Alliance – Cloud Control Matrix

The Cloud Control Matrix (CCM) is a cybersecurity framework developed by the Cloud Security Alliance (CSA) that provides a standardized approach for evaluating the security of cloud computing services. CCM can be used to implement a zero-trust network architecture by providing a comprehensive set of security controls and standards that can be applied to cloud-based resources and services.

One of the key benefits of CCM in the context of zero-trust networking is that it provides a comprehensive framework for evaluating the security of cloud-based resources and services. By leveraging CCM, administrators can ensure that cloud-based resources and services meet the necessary security standards and controls to support a zero-trust architecture.

CCM can also provide guidance on how to implement granular access controls and authentication mechanisms that are tied to user identity and context. By following CCM standards and controls, administrators can ensure that users are who they claim to be, and that they are only granted access to resources and applications that they are authorized to access.

Another benefit of CCM in the context of zero-trust networking is that it can help reduce the attack surface of the network. By implementing CCM security controls and standards, administrators can limit the potential for unauthorized access and data breaches in cloud-based resources and services.

Overall, CCM can be a valuable tool for implementing zero-trust networking, providing a standardized approach for evaluating and implementing security controls in cloud-based resources and services. By leveraging the guidance and controls provided by CCM, administrators can more easily implement a zero-trust architecture and protect against advanced threats.

7.10 PCI DSS

PCI DSS (Payment Card Industry Data Security Standard) and zero-trust are two distinct but related concepts in the field of cybersecurity. Here's an overview of each concept:

- PCI DSS (Payment Card Industry Data Security Standard):
    - PCI DSS is a set of security standards established by the Payment Card Industry Security Standards Council (PCI SSC). It applies to organizations that handle credit card transactions and aims to protect the cardholder data and ensure the security of the payment card ecosystem. Compliance with PCI DSS is mandatory for organizations that accept, process, store, or transmit credit card information.

- Key features of PCI DSS include:
    - Data protection: PCI DSS provides guidelines for the secure handling of cardholder data, including encryption, access controls, and network segmentation.
    - Network security: It emphasizes the implementation of robust network security measures, such as firewalls, secure configurations, and regular network monitoring.
    - Access controls: PCI DSS requires organizations to restrict access to cardholder data based on a need-to-know basis, implement unique user IDs, and regularly review user access privileges.
    - Regular testing: Organizations must conduct regular vulnerability scans and penetration tests to identify and address security vulnerabilities.
    - Security policies: PCI DSS mandates the development and implementation of comprehensive security policies and procedures that address various aspects of data security and access controls.

PCI DSS has recently been released in version 4.0, with both changes and new requirements. Some of the new requirements are:

- Security methods must develop as threats change to continue to fulfill the security needs of the payments industry.
    - The requirements for multi-factor authentication (MFA) are more stringent.
    - Password requirements have been updated.
    - To address current concerns, new e-commerce and phishing standards have been implemented.
- New requirements have been added with an ongoing understanding of security to promote security as a continuous process.
    - Assigned roles and responsibilities for each requirement.
    - Adding guidance to help people better understand how to implement and maintain security.
    - The new reporting option highlights areas for improvement and provides greater transparency for report reviewers.
- Added new requirements to enable more options and support payment technology innovation to increase flexibility for organizations using different methods to achieve their security goals.
    - Permissions for the group, shared, and public accounts.
    - Targeted risk analyses aim to enable organizations to establish the frequency of performing certain activities.
    - A customized approach, a new way to enforce and validate PCI DSS requirements, gives organizations another option that uses innovative methods to achieve their security goals.
- Detailed verification and reporting options have been developed to improve verification methods and procedures.

- Increased congruence between information reported in a compliance report or self-assessment questionnaire and information summarized in the attestation of compliance.

7.11 Zero-trust Tooling

It might seem strange to talk about tooling in a governance chapter, but a lot of the tools needed for a zero-trust implementation have their own governance needs.

There are several tools available for organizations to implement a zero-trust security model, including:

1. Identity and access management (IAM) solutions: IAM solutions provide centralized management of user identities and access to information and resources, including multi-factor authentication, password management, and the use of identity management systems.
2. Network security tools: Network security tools, such as firewalls, intrusion detection systems, and virtual private networks (VPNs), provide network-level security controls for monitoring and controlling network traffic.
3. Data security tools: Data security tools, such as data encryption, data loss prevention (DLP), and data backup and recovery, provide data-level security controls for protecting sensitive information.
4. Endpoint security tools: Endpoint security tools, such as antivirus software, endpoint detection and response (EDR) systems, and device management systems, provide security controls for protecting endpoints, such as computers and mobile devices.
5. Application security tools: Application security tools, such as web application firewalls (WAFs), application whitelisting, and secure software development practices, provide security controls for protecting applications and the data they access.
6. Security information and event management (SIEM) systems: SIEM systems provide centralized management and analysis of security events, including the detection of security incidents, the identification of security threats, and the management of security alerts.
7. Micro-segmentation solutions: Micro-segmentation solutions provide granular network segmentation, allowing organizations to isolate and secure critical resources and applications within their network.

Each of these tools, when looked at as stand alone, needs to have good governance in place in order to be effective. Identity for instance, I cannot count the number of times I have done assessments for clients and found old or stale accounts in their identity management systems.

In the case of VPN, I have found implementations out there using vulnerable encryption algorithms, because the VPNs have not been maintained regularly. Both cases are textbook examples of weak processes and governance for the infrastructure.

7.12 Zero-trust Maintenance

Maintaining a zero-trust security model requires continuous monitoring, assessment, and improvement of the security controls and processes in place. Here are some steps organizations can follow to maintain a zero-trust security model:

1. Monitor and assess security controls: Regularly monitor and assess the effectiveness of the security controls in place, including identity and access management (IAM) solutions, network security tools, data security tools, endpoint security tools, and application security tools.
2. Continuously verify and authenticate access: Continuously verify and authenticate all requests for access to information and resources, using multi-factor authentication, password management, and identity management systems.
3. Conduct regular security audits: Conduct regular security audits to identify potential vulnerabilities and ensure that security controls are aligned with best practices and industry standards.
4. Review and update security policies and procedures: Regularly review and update security policies and procedures, including incident response plans, to ensure that they are up-to-date and aligned with the evolving security landscape.
5. Implement software updates and patches: Regularly implement software updates and patches for security tools, applications, and operating systems to address potential vulnerabilities.
6. Monitor and respond to security incidents: Monitor and respond to security incidents in a timely manner, using security information and event management (SIEM) systems, incident response plans, and incident response teams.
7. Continuously educate employees: Continuously educate employees on security best practices and the importance of following security policies and procedures.

By following these steps, organizations can maintain their zero-trust security implementation and reduce the risk of security incidents. Remember, however, it is of the utmost importance to remember that the security landscape is constantly evolving, and organizations must continuously monitor, assess, and improve their security controls and processes.

7.13 The Art of War

No, I am not going to begin talking about zero-trust in a cyber war context, but the original treatise from Sun Tzu does contain some good advice, as it relates to cybersecurity. War is conflict, and cybersecurity is a conflict between us, the defenders, and the attackers that want to compromise our security. This makes the original work relevant in a modern cybersecurity context.

The principles outlined in "The Art of War" can be applied to the implementation and maintenance of a zero-trust security model. Here are a few ways in which the principles of "The Art of War" can be applied to zero-trust:

1. Know your enemy: In the context of zero-trust, it is important to understand the types of threats and attack vectors that exist, so that organizations can implement appropriate security controls and respond to incidents in a timely manner.

2. Plan and prepare for the worst-case scenario: Organizations should plan for potential security incidents and prepare for the worst-case scenario by implementing incident response plans, training employees on security best practices, and regularly reviewing and updating security policies and procedures.

3. Anticipate your opponent's moves: By continuously monitoring and assessing the effectiveness of security controls, organizations can anticipate potential security incidents and respond to them before they cause significant harm.

4. Be flexible and adaptable: The security landscape is constantly evolving, and organizations must be flexible and adaptable in order to stay ahead of potential threats. Regularly monitoring, assessing, and improving security controls and processes can help organizations maintain a zero-trust security model in the face of evolving threats.

5. Use deception: In a zero-trust security model, organizations can use deception to mislead potential attackers and protect sensitive information. For example, organizations can use honeypots, decoy systems, and fake data to distract and mislead potential attackers.

This concludes this chapter on governance and compliance for zero trust. Please do not underestimate the importance of the principles outlined here! Good governance benefits, not just cybersecurity, but the business and organization overall.

8

OT Zero-trust Security

Operational technology (OT), sometimes called industrial control systems (ICS) or SCADA (supervisory control and data acquisition systems) will not be known to everyone, I will therefore begin this chapter with an introduction to the terminologies used within OT, along with information on context for the uses of the terms.

Before doing that, however, I will spend a few lines explaining the importance of security for the OT infrastructures in use around the world. Operational technology (OT) refers to the hardware and software systems used to control and monitor industrial processes, physical infrastructure, and production facilities. It is a business-critical component of many industries, such as manufacturing, energy, transportation, and communication.

The importance of OT lies in its ability to automate and control various processes and equipment, leading to improved efficiency, safety, and reliability. Here are a few examples:

1. Improved efficiency: OT systems can automate many manual processes, reducing the need for manual labor and improving productivity. This leads to increased efficiency and reduced costs.

2. Improved safety: OT systems monitor and control industrial processes, ensuring that equipment operates within safe parameters. This helps reduce the risk of accidents, equipment damage, and environmental hazards.

3. Reliability: OT systems can detect and diagnose equipment problems in real time, allowing for quick resolution and reducing downtime. This leads to improved reliability and availability of critical systems and equipment.

4. Increased visibility: OT systems provide real-time data on the status and performance of equipment, allowing operators to make informed decisions and take corrective action when necessary.

The one of the most recent examples of a critical OT system getting attacked and made unavailable for the purpose it was designed for is the Colonial Oil Pipeline attack that happened back in May of 2021, which resulted in long queues at the petrol stations around the United States. Attacks against OT systems will in many cases have an immediate and serious impact on societies. Hence the importance of cybersecurity of OT infrastructures.

Operational technology, or OT as I refer to it in this chapter, arrived on the cyber security scene in a big way back in 2010 when Stuxnet arrived as the first real example of cyberwar between two countries. Stuxnet was designed to sabotage the Iranian nuclear program by attacking the Siemens OT equipment in use at the enrichment sites in Iran. Enrichment is the way uranium is made ready for nuclear reactors, or nuclear weapons.

This made the vulnerabilities in ordinary OT infrastructures a major concern for all, because if an OT infrastructure secured like the Iranian one could be attacked, then what about the more civilian OT infrastructures?

8.1 Terminology

Before beginning the zero-trust part of this chapter, I will begin by establishing some of the terminology of OT, for those of you that are new to cybersecurity within OT infrastructures. The most common terms are listed in Table 8.1.

Table 8.1: The most common terms in OT.

Term	Explanation
SCADA	Supervisory control and data acquisition (SCADA) is a control system architecture comprising computers, networked data communications and graphical user interfaces for high-level supervision of machines and processes. It also covers sensors and other devices, such as programmable logic controllers, which interface with process plant or machinery.
PLC	A programmable logic controller (PLC) or programmable controller is an industrial computer that has been ruggedized and adapted for the control of manufacturing processes, such as assembly lines, machines, robotic devices, or any activity that requires high reliability, ease of programming, and process fault diagnosis.
ICS	An industrial control system (ICS) is an electronic control system and associated instrumentation used for industrial process control. Control systems can range in size from a few modular panel-mounted controllers to large interconnected and interactive distributed control systems (DCSs) with many thousands of field connections. Control systems receive data from remote sensors measuring process variables (PVs), compare the collected data with desired setpoints (SPs), and derive command functions that are used to control a process through the final control elements (FCEs), such as control valves.

Table 8.1: Continued

Term	Explanation
OT	Operational technology (OT) is hardware and software that detects or causes a change, through the direct monitoring and/or control of industrial equipment, assets, processes and events. The term has become established to demonstrate the technological and functional differences between traditional information technology (IT) systems and industrial control systems environment, the so-called "IT in the non-carpeted areas".
IIoT	The industrial internet of things (IIoT) refers to interconnected sensors, instruments, and other devices networked together with computers' industrial applications, including manufacturing and energy management. This connectivity allows for data collection, exchange, and analysis, potentially facilitating improvements in productivity and efficiency as well as other economic benefits. The IIoT is an evolution of a distributed control system (DCS) that allows for a higher degree of automation by using cloud computing to refine and optimize the process controls.
DCS	A distributed control system (DCS) is a computerized control system for a process or plant usually with many control loops, in which autonomous controllers are distributed throughout the system, but there is no central operator supervisory control. This contrasts with systems that use centralized controllers; either discrete controllers located at a central control room or within a central computer. The DCS concept increases reliability and reduces installation costs by localizing control functions near the process plant, with remote monitoring and supervision.

The PLC component of OT became infamous back in 2010 with the Stuxnet attack, since this was the main component attacked at the Iranian nuclear facility. You can see an example of a PLC in Figure 8.1.

Figure 8.1: PLCs are the worker units in an OT infrastructure and must be protected from malicious traffic, since many of them are old and not designed for today's threats.

The communications protocols in use with OT environments also differ from the TCP/IP we know from IT systems. The Table 8.2 lists some of these protocols and their uses.

Table 8.2: Some protocols and their uses.

Protocol	Explanation
Modbus	Modbus is a data communications protocol originally published by Modicon (now Schneider Electric) in 1979 for use with its programmable logic controllers (PLCs). Modbus has become a de facto standard communication protocol and is now a commonly available means of connecting industrial electronic devices.
Profinet	Profinet (usually styled as PROFINET, as a portmanteau for process field network) is an industry technical standard for data communication over industrial Ethernet, designed for collecting data from, and controlling equipment in, industrial systems, with a particular strength in delivering data under tight time constraints. The standard is maintained and supported by Profibus and Profinet International, an umbrella organization headquartered in Karlsruhe, Germany.
OSGP	The Open Smart Grid Protocol (OSGP) is a family of specifications published by the European Telecommunications Standards Institute (ETSI) used in conjunction with the ISO/IEC 14908 control networking standard for smart grid applications. OSGP is optimized to provide reliable and efficient delivery of command-and-control information for smart meters, direct load control modules, solar panels, gateways, and other smart grid devices. With over 5 million OSGP based smart meters and devices deployed worldwide it is one of the most widely used smart meter and smart grid device networking standards.
Instabus	Instabus, is a decentralized open system to manage and control electrical devices within a facility. It was developed by Berker, Gira, Jung, Merten and Siemens AG. There are about 200 companies of electrical supplies using this communication protocol. The European Installation Bus (EIB) allows all electrical components to be interconnected through an electrical bus. Every component is able to send commands to other components, no matter where they are. A typical EIB network is made of electrical components such as switches, pulsers, electric motors, electro valves, contactors, and sensors.

There are many, many more protocols than the ones listed above, and although the industry is slowly but surely moving to Ethernet as the underlying protocol for communication with devices in an OT infrastructure, legacy communication will persist in many OT infrastructures for many years, due to the length of time a production plant will exist, before the technology gets upgraded.

8.2 IT/OT

The reason for the focus in recent years, on the vulnerabilities of OT, is because of the integration that is rapidly happening between IT and OT infrastructures (Figure 8.3). This integration makes it possible for nefarious hackers to make the jump from the regular IT systems, to attack the OT infrastructures. This, along with the fact that in many cases IT is being used to manage and measure

OT systems, makes OT vulnerable to the same attacks that we have seen on IT infrastructures for decades.

OT (operational technology) and IT (information technology) are two different types of systems that require different approaches to cybersecurity.

OT refers to systems that are used to monitor and control physical processes in industries such as manufacturing, energy, and transportation. These systems are often embedded in physical devices such as sensors, controllers, and actuators. Examples of OT systems include industrial control systems (ICS), supervisory control and data acquisition (SCADA) systems, and programmable logic controllers (PLC).

IT, on the other hand, refers to systems used for data processing, storage, and communication. IT systems include desktop computers, servers, networks, and software applications.

Because OT and IT systems have different purposes and functions, they have different cybersecurity requirements (Figure 8.2). OT systems are designed to be highly reliable and available, but they may not have strong security measures in place. IT systems, on the other hand, are often designed with strong security measures in mind, but they may not be optimized for reliability and availability.

Figure 8.2: The recent integration between OT and IT has created a new set of threats that cybersecurity professionals must account for.

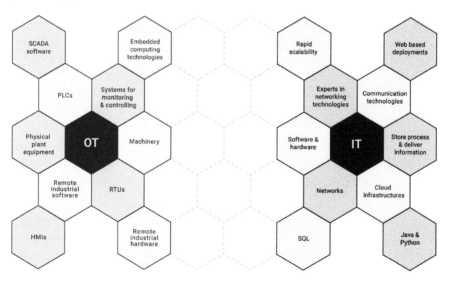

These challenges, and the disparate groups of staff responsible for managing them, has resulted in a kind of conflict between the engineers responsible for the OT infrastructures, where the main focus is on up-time, and the cybersecurity engineers that are focused on securing the various infrastructures.

Remember, many OT infrastructures are no longer maintained by the original vendor behind the components in the infrastructure, since a factory might have been built decades ago. The components in the factory cannot be "patched" as we are used to, because when the component was built way back when, patching was not a consideration for OT equipment.

Operational technology (OT) security maintenance ensures that the systems and processes that control and monitor industrial processes and critical infrastructure are secure and up to date. OT systems include things like supervisory control and data acquisition (SCADA) systems, programmable logic controllers (PLCs), and other control systems that are used to manage and automate industrial processes.

Here are some key practices for maintaining OT security:

1. Patching and updates: Keep all OT systems up to date with the latest security patches and updates. This is crucial for protecting against known vulnerabilities and exploits.
2. Access control: Limit access to OT systems to authorized personnel only. Use strong passwords and multi-factor authentication to ensure that only authorized users can access sensitive systems and data.
3. Network segmentation: Segment OT networks from other networks and limit access between them. This can help prevent attacks from spreading from one part of the network to another.
4. Monitoring and alerting: Implement monitoring and alerting tools to detect unusual activity on OT systems. This can help identify potential attacks before they can cause significant damage.
5. Incident response planning: Have a plan in place to respond to security incidents. This should include procedures for identifying, containing, and remedying security breaches.
6. Regular assessments: Conduct regular security assessments to identify potential vulnerabilities and areas for improvement in OT security.

By following these practices, organizations can help ensure the security and reliability of their OT systems, reducing the risk of cyber-attacks and other security incidents that could impact critical infrastructure and industrial processes.

Note that many of the steps above mirror the ones we are used to in an IT environment. It is because of the lifetime of OT equipment that we cannot just apply these steps to all of the legacy equipment in use out in the world. The OT vendors have begun creating equipment that can be protected with the usual steps we know from IT, patching and the like, but we will for many years have to contend with a large amount of OT infrastructures that simply cannot be patched as we are used to.

Figure 8.3: Integration OT and IT creates complexity, and this complexity must be managed in order for us to secure the OT environments.

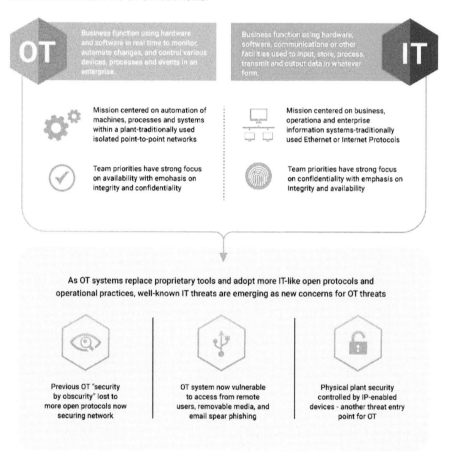

8.3 OT Security Frameworks

There are several frameworks for cybersecurity in an industrial setting. This section lists the two most important ones in my opinion.

8.3.1 Purdue Enterprise Reference Architecture

The Purdue Enterprise Reference Architecture (PERA) is a framework for designing and organizing industrial automation systems. It was developed by the Purdue University in the 1990s and has since been widely adopted in the manufacturing and process industries.

PERA is a hierarchical model that organizes an industrial automation system into levels. Each level has a specific role and communicates with the adjacent levels. The levels are as follows:

Level 0: The physical process.

Level 1: The control level, which monitors and controls the physical process.

Level 2: The supervisory level, which oversees the control level and provides information to higher levels.

Level 3: The production planning level, which plans and schedules the production process.

Level 4: The business planning level, which handles the overall business strategy and goals.

The levels are connected by a communication network that allows for the exchange of data and information between them. The network may include various protocols and technologies, such as Ethernet, TCP/IP, and OPC.

PERA provides a standardized approach for designing and implementing industrial automation systems. It helps to ensure that the system is scalable, modular, and maintainable. It also promotes interoperability and communication between different systems and components.

Overall, PERA is a useful tool for organizations that want to optimize their industrial automation systems and improve their operational efficiency.

8.3.2 IEC 62443

IEC 62443 is an international standard for cybersecurity in industrial automation and control systems (IACS). The standard was developed by the International Electrotechnical Commission (IEC) in response to the growing threat of cyber-attacks on industrial systems.

IEC 62443 consists of a series of standards and technical reports that provide guidelines for implementing cybersecurity measures in IACS. The standard covers various aspects of cybersecurity, including risk assessment, security policies, network security, access control, and incident response.

The standard defines four levels of security, with each level representing a different degree of cybersecurity. The levels are as follows:

Level 1: Basic security measures, suitable for systems with low cybersecurity requirements.

Level 2: Medium security measures, suitable for systems with moderate cybersecurity requirements.

Level 3: High security measures, suitable for systems with high cybersecurity requirements.

Level 4: Very high security measures, suitable for systems with extremely high cybersecurity requirements.

IEC 62443 is widely used by organizations in the manufacturing, energy, and transportation sectors, among others, to improve the cybersecurity of their industrial systems. By following the guidelines in the standard, organizations can reduce the risk of cyber-attacks, protect critical infrastructure, and ensure the safe and reliable operation of their industrial systems.

8.4 OT Zero-Trust

Zero trust can provide several benefits in operational technology (OT) environments, which are typically used in industrial control systems (ICS) and supervisory control and data acquisition (SCADA) systems.

1. Improved security posture: Zero trust assumes no trust, so all devices and users are treated as potential threats until they are properly authenticated and authorized. This can help to prevent unauthorized access to OT systems, which can have severe consequences, such as physical harm to personnel, environmental damage, or financial loss.
2. Segmentation and micro-segmentation: OT systems often have complex and interconnected networks that can make it difficult to implement effective security controls. Zero trust can help by providing segmentation and micro-segmentation capabilities, which can limit the attack surface and reduce the impact of any potential security breaches.
3. Granular access control: Zero-trust provides granular access control capabilities, which can limit access to specific resources and data based on the user's role and responsibilities. This

can help to prevent unauthorized access to sensitive information, such as intellectual property, trade secrets, or personal information.

4. Visibility and monitoring: Zero-trust provides visibility and monitoring capabilities that can help to detect and respond to security incidents in real time. This can help to prevent or limit the impact of security breaches and ensure that critical OT systems remain operational.

5. Compliance: OT environments are often subject to strict regulations and compliance requirements, such as the North American Electric Reliability Corporation Critical Infrastructure Protection (NERC CIP) standards. Zero trust can help organizations to meet these requirements by providing a comprehensive security framework that addresses key security principles, such as authentication, authorization, and accountability.

Zero-trust security is becoming increasingly important in operational technology (OT) environments because of the unique security risks posed by these systems. Unlike traditional IT networks, OT systems are often more vulnerable to cyber-attacks because they were not designed with security in mind and in many cases rely on outdated technology.

Zero-trust security takes the approach of assuming that no user or device can be trusted and requires verification of all access requests regardless of whether the user or device is inside or outside of the network perimeter. This approach helps to protect against both internal and external threats, as it requires authentication and authorization for all access to sensitive systems and data.

Implementing zero-trust security in an OT environment can help to prevent unauthorized access to critical infrastructure and control systems, reduce the risk of cyber-attacks and data breaches, and improve overall security posture. Zero-trust security can also help to detect and respond to security incidents quickly, by providing real-time monitoring and alerts for unusual or suspicious activity.

8.4.1 Purdue Enterprise Reference Architecture

The Purdue Enterprise Reference Architecture (PERA) and zero trust are two different concepts that can be used together to improve the cybersecurity of industrial automation systems.

PERA provides a framework for organizing industrial automation systems into different levels and defining the communication between those levels. This helps to improve the security of the system by isolating different levels and limiting the communication between them.

Zero trust, on the other hand, is a security model that assumes that all devices, users, and processes are potentially malicious and should not be trusted by default. Under the zero-trust model, access to resources is only granted after proper authentication and authorization, and all access requests are continuously monitored and analyzed for potential threats.

By combining PERA and zero-trust, industrial organizations can create a highly secure and resilient system. The PERA framework can be used to isolate and limit the communication between different levels of the system, while the zero-trust model can be used to ensure that all access to resources is properly authenticated and authorized.

In this approach, each level of the system would have its own security perimeter, and access between those perimeters would only be granted after proper authentication and authorization. This helps to reduce the risk of unauthorized access or data breaches, and it also makes it easier to identify and contain potential threats.

Overall, the combination of PERA and zero trust can provide a powerful and effective approach to securing industrial automation systems and protecting critical infrastructure from cyber-attacks.

1. Identify systems and assets: Identify all IACS systems and assets in the environment and classify them according to the PERA model. This will help to determine the appropriate security controls and access requirements for each system and asset.

2. Conduct a risk assessment: Conduct a risk assessment to identify potential threats and vulnerabilities to the IACS environment. This will help to determine the appropriate security controls and access requirements needed to mitigate identified risks.

3. Establish security requirements: Use the PERA model to establish security requirements for each level of the IACS environment, based on the identified risks and assets. This should include a zero-trust security model that requires authentication and authorization for all access to sensitive systems and data.

4. Implement a zero-trust security model: Implement a zero-trust security model that includes the following:

   - Strong authentication mechanisms, such as multi-factor authentication, for all users and devices.
   - Role-based access controls to ensure that users have only the access they need to perform their jobs.
   - Network segmentation to limit access between systems and networks, and to isolate critical systems from less critical ones.
   - Monitoring and analyzing all traffic in the IACS environment for anomalous behavior or suspicious activity.

- Using encryption and other security technologies to protect data in transit and at rest.
- Test and validate: Test and validate the security measures implemented in the IACS environment to ensure that they are effective and meet the security requirements established in step 3.

By using the PERA model to establish security requirements and implementing a zero-trust security model in IACS environments, organizations can help ensure that their critical infrastructure and industrial processes remain secure and reliable.

8.4.2 IEC 62443

IEC 62443 and zero trust are two approaches to cybersecurity that can be used together to provide a comprehensive security solution.

IEC 62443 is a series of international standards that provide guidelines for securing industrial automation and control systems. The standards provide a framework for identifying and managing cybersecurity risks in IACS environments, and cover areas such as network security, access control, incident response, and system development.

Zero trust, on the other hand, is a security model that assumes that all users, devices, and network traffic are potentially malicious, and requires verification of all access requests regardless of whether they are coming from inside or outside the network perimeter. This approach helps to minimize the attack surface by only granting access on a need-to-know basis and using strong authentication and encryption.

When used together, IEC 62443 and zero trust can provide a strong defense-in-depth approach to cybersecurity. IEC 62443 provides a framework for securing IACS systems, while zero trust provides a methodology for implementing a strong access control model that assumes that all users and devices are potentially malicious.

Some key considerations for implementing IEC 62443 and zero trust together include:

- Conducting a risk assessment to identify the key assets and threats to IACS systems.
- Implementing a defense-in-depth strategy that includes both network and system security measures.
- Segregating IACS networks from enterprise networks to reduce the attack surface.
- Using strong access controls and authentication mechanisms, such as multi-factor authentication, to verify all access requests.

- Implementing strong encryption mechanisms to protect sensitive data and network traffic.
- Regularly monitoring and auditing access requests and system activity to detect anomalies and potential threats.

By using IEC 62433 as a framework for establishing security requirements and implementing a zero-trust security model, organizations can help ensure that their OT environments are protected against cyber threats and that critical infrastructure and industrial processes remain secure and reliable.

There is a significant overlap between the Purdue model and IEC 62443, but the most modern and well-maintained framework is the IEC 62443 one, and it is this framework that is the main focus for both vendors and organizations challenged with the new focus on cybersecurity for OT infrastructures.

8.5 OT Security Training/Certification

Unfortunately, there are not a lot of possibilities for training in OT security. There is no formal training within the various educational institutions around the world, but I will still use this last part of the chapter to point you to some resources, in case OT cybersecurity speaks to you as a career path.

8.5.1 International Society of Automation (ISA)

ISA provides formal training course in cybersecurity for OT environments, based on IEC 62443:

Certificate 1: ISA/IEC 62443 Cybersecurity Fundamentals Specialist

Certificate 2: ISA/IEC 62443 Cybersecurity Risk Assessment Specialist

Certificate 3: ISA/IEC 62443 Cybersecurity Design Specialist

Certificate 4: ISA/IEC 62443 Cybersecurity Maintenance Specialist

ISA/IEC 62443 Cybersecurity Expert: Individuals who achieve Certificates 1, 2, 3, and 4 are designated as ISA/IEC 62443 Cybersecurity Experts.

The above courses can be taken as online training on-demand, or in person classes. If you are a member of ISA, there is a reduction in the price! www.isa.org

8.5.2 GIAC

GIAC has for many years been seen as a core certification/training provider for serious cyber professionals, and they of course have certifications on OT security as well:

- Global Industrial Cyber Security Professional (GICSP)
    - o Industrial control system components, purposes, deployments, significant drivers, and constraints
    - o Control system attack surfaces, methods, and tools
    - o Control system approaches to system and network defense architectures and techniques
    - o Incident-response skills in a control system environment
    - o Governance models and resources for industrial cybersecurity professionals.
- GIAC Response and Industrial Defense (GRID)
    - o Active Defense Concepts and Application, Detection and Analysis in an ICS environment
    - o Discovery and Monitoring in an ICS environment, ICS-focused Digital Forensics, and ICS-focused Incident Response
    - o Malware Analysis Techniques, Threat Analysis in an ICS environment, and Threat Intelligence Fundamentals.
- GIAC Critical Infrastructure Protection (GCIP)
    - o BES cyber system identification and strategies for lowering their impact rating
    - o Nuances of NERC defined terms and CIP standards applicability
    - o Strategic implementation approaches for supporting technologies
    - o Recurring tasks and strategies for CIP program maintenance.

The above certifications and training are vendor neutral, but there is cybersecurity specific training available from most of the OT vendors out there focusing on their own equipment. Depending on the organization where you might become responsible for the security of the OT infrastructure, these courses might provide value to you as well!

9

Next Steps

This book has touched on many, many subjects, all of which are important to a zero-trust project. I hope that you have gotten the message of the complexity of implementing zero trust in an existing infrastructure. That is not to say that the effort is not worth the resources, time and money needed, not at all! Let's review the topics we have been looking into.

9.1 Cisco

Cisco offers a range of solutions that can be used to implement zero-trust security in networks. These solutions are designed to provide granular access control and protect against unauthorized access to network resources and data. Here are some of the ways Cisco implements zero trust:

- Network segmentation: Cisco offers network segmentation solutions, such as Software-Defined Access (SD-Access) and Cisco TrustSec, that can be used to enforce zero-trust policies. These solutions can segment the network into smaller, more manageable pieces, allowing organizations to limit access to sensitive data and resources.
- Identity-based access control: Cisco offers solutions such as Cisco Identity Services Engine (ISE) and Cisco Duo that provide identity-based access control. These solutions can verify the identity of users and devices before granting access to the network.
- Continuous monitoring: Cisco offers solutions such as Cisco Stealthwatch that provide continuous monitoring of the network. These solutions can detect and respond to security incidents in real-time, helping organizations to prevent or limit the impact of security breaches.

- Analytics and automation: Cisco offers solutions such as Cisco SecureX that provide analytics and automation capabilities. These solutions can help organizations to identify security threats and automate responses to security incidents, improving the overall security posture.
- Integration: Cisco offers solutions that integrate with other security technologies, such as firewalls and endpoint protection, to provide a comprehensive zero-trust security framework.

Cisco is a leading provider of networking solutions, and its solutions can be used to implement the networking layer of a zero-trust security model. The networking layer of zero trust is focused on implementing network segmentation and micro-segmentation to limit access to specific resources and data.

1. Comprehensive solutions: Cisco offers a range of solutions that can be used to implement network segmentation and micro-segmentation, including Software-Defined Access (SD-Access) and Cisco TrustSec. These solutions are designed to provide granular access control and protect against unauthorized access to network resources and data.
2. Identity-based access control: Cisco solutions such as Cisco Identity Services Engine (ISE) and Cisco Duo provide identity-based access control, which can verify the identity of users and devices before granting access to the network. This helps to ensure that only authorized users and devices are accessing network resources.
3. Continuous monitoring: Cisco solutions such as Cisco Stealthwatch provide continuous monitoring of the network. These solutions can detect and respond to security incidents in real time, helping organizations to prevent or limit the impact of security breaches.
4. Integration: Cisco solutions integrate with other security technologies, such as firewalls and endpoint protection, to provide a comprehensive zero-trust security framework. This allows organizations to leverage their existing security investments and build a more effective security architecture.
5. Experience and expertise: Cisco have a wealth of experience and expertise in networking and security, and its solutions are widely used by organizations around the world. This means that organizations can rely on Cisco for support and expertise in implementing zero-trust security at the networking layer.

9.2 Microsoft/Cloud

I have touched on multiple Microsoft tools in this book, most prominently Azure AD and Azure itself. Microsoft provides a range of solutions that can be used to implement a zero-trust security model. These solutions are designed to provide granular access control and protect against unauthorized access to network resources and data.

- Identity and access management: Microsoft offers solutions such as Azure Active Directory (AD) and Microsoft Identity Manager (MIM) that provide identity and access management capabilities.

These solutions can help to verify the identity of users and devices before granting access to network resources.

- Conditional access: Microsoft offers conditional access capabilities within Azure AD, which allows organizations to control access to resources based on risk and compliance policies. This helps to ensure that only authorized users and devices are accessing network resources.
- Endpoint protection: Microsoft offers solutions such as Microsoft Defender for Endpoint that provide endpoint protection capabilities. These solutions can detect and respond to security threats on endpoints, helping to prevent or limit the impact of security breaches.
- Cloud security: Microsoft provides a range of cloud security solutions, such as Azure Security Center and Microsoft Cloud App Security, that can be used to implement zero trust in cloud environments. These solutions provide visibility and control over cloud resources and data, helping to ensure that they are secure.
- Integration: Microsoft solutions integrate with other security technologies, such as firewalls and endpoint protection, to provide a comprehensive zero-trust security framework. This allows organizations to leverage their existing security investments and build a more effective security architecture.

Most of the tools above can be used across the Microsoft cloud environment, Azure, M365 and Dynamics 365. As mentioned in the chapter on Cloud and zero-trust, many companies are utilizing multiple different clouds from different vendors in their business environments. This presents some new challenges and risks to businesses and organizations.

1. Lack of visibility: Multi-cloud environments can make it difficult to gain visibility of all of the cloud resources that are being used by an organization. This can make it difficult to identify security risks and respond to security incidents.
2. Complexity: Multi-cloud environments can be complex, with different cloud providers and services having different security configurations and controls. This can make it challenging to maintain a consistent security posture across all cloud resources.
3. Data protection: Multi-cloud environments can create challenges around data protection. Data may be stored in different clouds, and it may be difficult to ensure consistent data protection policies and controls across all clouds.
4. Compliance: Multi-cloud environments can create compliance challenges, as different clouds may have different compliance requirements. It may be difficult to ensure that all clouds are compliant with relevant regulations and standards.
5. Unauthorized access: Multi-cloud environments can be more vulnerable to unauthorized access, as there may be more points of entry for attackers. It can be challenging to ensure that only authorized users and devices are accessing cloud resources.
6. Cloud provider security: Cloud providers may have different levels of security, and it can be challenging to ensure that they are all secure. Organizations may need to perform due diligence on cloud providers to ensure that they have appropriate security controls in place.

Governance across multiple different clouds presents some challenges as well, since in many cases the governance models differ between cloud vendors.

9.3 Governance

Governance plays a critical role in implementing and maintaining a zero-trust security model. Zero trust is a security model that assumes no trust, whether inside or outside the network, and provides granular access control based on user authentication and authorization. Governance ensures that security policies and procedures are aligned with business objectives and that compliance with relevant regulations and standards is maintained.

- Risk assessment: Conduct a risk assessment to identify potential security risks and vulnerabilities in the network. This assessment should consider all types of threats, including insider threats, external threats, and supply chain risks.
- Policy development: Develop policies and procedures that align with business objectives and address the identified security risks. These policies should include access control policies, data protection policies, incident response procedures, and training programs for employees.
- Compliance monitoring: Monitor compliance with relevant regulations and standards, such as GDPR or HIPAA, and implement controls to ensure that data privacy and security requirements are met.
- Continuous monitoring: Implement continuous monitoring of the network to detect and respond to security incidents in real time. This monitoring should include network traffic analysis, threat detection, and security incident management.
- Vendor management: Implement a vendor management program to ensure that third-party vendors and suppliers are meeting security and privacy requirements. This program should include due diligence assessments, vendor risk assessments, and contract management procedures.
- Metrics and reporting: Establish metrics and reporting mechanisms to measure the effectiveness of the zero-trust security model. These metrics should include measures of access control effectiveness, incident response time, and compliance with relevant regulations and standards.

I cannot overstress the importance of having good governance in place, in any organization, but it is especially important to zero trust, since without it, zero trust will fizzle out and the investment and benefits will disappear!

9.4 5G

5G networks play a critical role in supporting critical infrastructure and communications between individuals and need to be secure to protect against cyber threats. Zero trust is a security model that can be implemented in 5G networks to provide granular access control and ensure the security of network resources and data. Here are some ways to implement zero trust in 5G networks:

- Network segmentation: Use network segmentation and micro-segmentation to limit access to specific network resources based on user identity and device characteristics. This can help to prevent unauthorized access and reduce the attack surface.
- Identity and access management: Implement a centralized identity and access management (IAM) solution that provides strong authentication and authorization controls for all network resources. This will help to ensure that only authorized users and devices are accessing network resources.
- Continuous monitoring: Implement continuous monitoring of the network to detect and respond to security incidents in real time. This can help to prevent or limit the impact of security breaches.
- Encryption and data protection: Implement encryption and data protection measures for network resources to ensure that data is protected both in transit and at rest.
- Cloud access security brokers (CASBs): Implement a CASB solution that provides visibility and control over cloud resources and data. This can help to ensure that cloud resources are being used in a compliant and secure manner.
- Compliance: Implement compliance measures to ensure that the 5G network is meeting regulatory requirements and industry standards. This includes implementing security controls, such as encryption, and performing regular security audits and assessments.

9.5 Operational Technology (OT)

Operational technology (OT) is an essential component of critical infrastructure, and it is critical to secure OT systems against cyber threats. Zero trust is a security model that can be implemented in OT environments to provide granular access control and ensure the security of network resources and data.

- Network segmentation: Use network segmentation and micro-segmentation to limit access to specific OT resources based on user identity and device characteristics. This can help to prevent unauthorized access and reduce the attack surface.
- Identity and access management: Implement a centralized identity and access management (IAM) solution that provides strong authentication and authorization controls for all OT resources. This will help to ensure that only authorized users and devices are accessing OT resources.
- Continuous monitoring: Implement continuous monitoring of the OT network to detect and respond to security incidents in real time. This can help to prevent or limit the impact of security breaches.
- Encryption and data protection: Implement encryption and data protection measures for OT resources to ensure that data is protected both in transit and at rest.

- Compliance: Implement compliance measures to ensure that the OT system is meeting regulatory requirements and industry standards. This includes implementing security controls, such as encryption, and performing regular security audits and assessments.
- Vendor management: Implement a vendor management program to ensure that third-party vendors and suppliers are meeting security and privacy requirements. This program should include due diligence assessments, vendor risk assessments, and contract management procedures.

Have you noticed the repetition of many steps across the different areas where zero trust can make a difference? Zero trust is just an implementation of already known technologies and design steps in a much more rigorous manner and in all layers of the infrastructure.

9.6 The Future of Zero Trust

The future of zero trust is promising, as organizations continue to face evolving security threats that require a more comprehensive and effective security posture.

1. Integration with other security solutions: As zero trust becomes more widely adopted, it will likely be integrated more closely with other security solutions, such as endpoint protection, cloud security, and identity and access management. This will allow for a more comprehensive and effective security posture, where multiple security solutions work together to protect against cyber threats.
2. Automation: Automation will likely play a bigger role in the implementation and operation of zero-trust security models. Automated security controls, such as automated segmentation of networks, will improve security and reduce the workload of security personnel. Automated security response will also help organizations respond to security incidents in real time, improving overall security.
3. Advanced AI and machine learning: AI and machine learning technologies will be leveraged to provide more advanced threat detection and response capabilities within zero-trust security models. These technologies will enable organizations to detect threats that would be difficult for humans to identify and respond to, as well as adapt to new threats as they emerge.
4. Blockchain integration: Blockchain technology may be leveraged to provide a more secure and tamper-proof authentication and authorization framework within zero-trust security models. Blockchain-based identity and access management systems could improve security by ensuring that user identities are tamper-proof and eliminating the need for third-party identity providers.
5. Expansion to IoT: Zero trust may be expanded to cover the Internet of Things (IoT), providing granular access control and security for IoT devices and networks. IoT devices are often vulnerable to cyber-attacks and can serve as a gateway for attackers to gain access to networks, making zero-trust security models a critical need in securing IoT environments.

6. Cloud-native zero trust: Cloud-native zero-trust solutions may emerge, providing a more cloud-centric approach to zero-trust security. These solutions will likely focus on cloud-specific threats and provide granular access control to cloud resources based on user identity and device characteristics.

Index